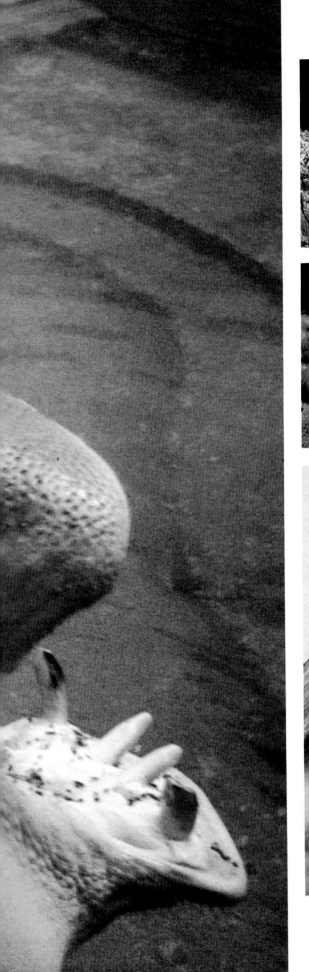

By
David Koul
age 8

A ZOO FOR ALL SEASONS
THE SMITHSONIAN ANIMAL WORLD

SMITHSONIAN EXPOSITION BOOKS

DISTRIBUTED TO THE TRADE BY
W.W. NORTON & COMPANY, NEW YORK, N.Y.

SECOND PRINTING

The Smithsonian Institution
Secretary, S. Dillon Ripley

The National Zoological Park
Director, Theodore H. Reed

Smithsonian Exposition Books
Director, James K. Page, Jr.
Senior Editor, Russell Bourne
Business Manager, Thomas A. Hoffman

Staff, A Zoo for All Seasons
Alfred Meyer, Editor
Bettie Loux Donley, Managing Editor
Caren W. Keshishian, Picture Editor
Amy Donovan, Assistant Editor
Ann Beasley, Production Editor
Patricia Upchurch, Editorial Assistant
Christine Nonnenmacher, Florence Blau,
June Armstrong, Francine Atwell, Assistants

William H. Kelty, Marketing Consultant

Writers: Thomas Crosby, Amy Donovan,
John F. Eisenberg, Janet L. Hopson,
Theodore H. Reed

Special photography by: William Albert
Allard, Steve Altman, Kenneth Garrett, Max
Hirshfeld, Susanne Page, Bill Weems

Illustrations by: Gloria Kamen, Marsha
Lederman

Index: Evelyn Sinclair

Design: Michael David Brown, Inc.
Michael David Brown, Art Direction
Assisted by Jeanne Clemente Kelly, Helen D.
B. Vickers

Separations and Engravings:
    Lanman Lithoplate, Inc.
Typography: VIP Systems, Inc.
Printing: Rand McNally and Company

Grateful acknowledgment is given to
Sybil Hamlet, Kathleen A. Lynch, Michael
Morgan, Pat Vosburgh, and to the staff of
the National Zoological Park and its
Conservation and Research Center at Front
Royal, Va., who assisted in the preparation of
this volume.

Library of Congress Number 79-52492
ISBN 0-89599-003-2

©1979 Smithsonian Institution

CONTENTS

Page 1: Endangered in its native Indonesia, the orangutan's name translates "man of the jungle." Page 2-3: Female Atlas lion tolerates the antics of one of her cubs. Page 4: A gaping maw often greets the visitor to the hippo enclosures. Page 5: Similarly sized by the magic of photography, the alligator snapping turtle, top, of the Mississippi River Delta, is several feet long, while the tokay gecko is but a few colorful inches. Bottom, a white pelican. Page 6: Top left, classic posture of an intent young zoo visitor. Zoo staff, top right, carefully crate a young giraffe for travel. Center left, keeper Larry Newman faces off with a prehensile-tailed porcupine. Young artist's portrait of a pelican, center right. Bottom left, a crowded Zoo on Easter weekend, and bottom right, Robert Mulcahy, Manager of Design, stencils crane prints on the walks. Page 7: Misnamed Marvin at birth, this cub developed into a Bengal tigress. Page 8: Zebras are not always black and white, but often shades of brown or chestnut as well. Page 9: A golden pheasant.

PENSI AND AZY

CRISIS AT THE ZOO

Thomas Crosby

When Melanie Bond arrived for work at the National Zoo shortly before 7 a.m. on July 7, 1976, she found Archie, a male orangutan, looking attentively through the peephole in his cage door into the adjoining cage of Pensi, a pregnant female orangutan.

Bond knew immediately that something out of the ordinary had occurred, because Archie usually slept until she arrived to begin her daily duties as one of the keepers of the great apes. Rushing to Pensi's cage, Bond saw the 150-pound orangutan lying in the right front corner. In her hairy, massive arms, she cradled a slightly undersized newborn infant.

News of the birth spread quickly among Zoo employees. Orangutan births in captivity are rare, but this one could prove even rarer as both parents had been born in captivity: Pensi at the Yerkes Regional Primate Research Center in Atlanta and Archie's son Atjeh at the National Zoo.

A highly endangered species, fewer than 3,000 orangutans are believed to still exist in the rain forests of Kalimantan and Sumatra, their native habitats. In 1978 there were fewer than 400 orangutans in zoos around the world. In the 70 years or so orangutans have been kept in captivity, there have been no fully documented second-generation births, although several successful matings have occurred between captive-born orangutans and wild-caught mates.

The excitement at the Zoo, therefore, was somewhat tempered by the knowledge that survival is especially precarious for newborn orangutans in captivity. The first offspring typically experience greater difficulties than subsequent ones, perhaps because of the inexperience of the mother.

Bond's watchful eye caused her to be less than optimistic at first. She noticed that the infant's grasping ability seemed weak, although Pensi kept a firm grip on her baby. Later in the day, however, Bond's anxiety eased when she was able to lure Pensi to the cage bars. She thought that the infant, apparently a female, looked healthy.

Bond, a diminutive 25-year-old, began observing daytime interaction between Pensi and her offspring, receiving help from a postdoctoral student from the Office of Zoological Research. No nighttime watches were scheduled for fear that a break in routine might upset Pensi. For the same reason the great ape section of the Small Mammal House, closed to the public on the day of the infant's birth, reopened 24 hours later.

Pensi proved to be an attentive mother in all ways but one: she did not sever the umbilical cord, which dragged around on the cage floor; and on at least one occasion she placed the baby over a shelf strut, supporting the entire weight of the infant by the umbilical cord. On the third day, shriveled and dried, the cord dropped off.

From the beginning the observers watched carefully to see if Pensi would nurse. Not once in 13 documented captive orangutan births at various zoos had an infant been seen nursing on the first day, though it remained unclear whether the delay resulted from the mother's shyness in the presence of human observers or simply from a natural lag between birth and the onset of lactation. During the daytime watches, neither Bond nor the others witnessed any nursing. They hoped Pensi was suckling her baby at night, when the great apes were alone with each other.

Midway through the fourth day, the drama ended. The tiny orangutan lay dead. Pensi, apparently trying to elicit some kind of vocal response from her inert daughter, started prodding the baby. Then she placed it stomach down over the shelf strut and began pulling its arms and legs.

Using a fire extinguisher and a water hose, keepers separated Pensi from the dead infant. A necropsy by the Zoo's Office of Pathology later showed that the orangutan had died from bacterial meningitis, possibly caused by bacteria that had entered the infant's circulatory system through the umbilicus.

Zoo staff immediately prepared a more elaborate plan for Pensi's next pregnancy, calling for removal of the infant from Pensi

At 5:30AM Walter Tucker, animal keeper, anxiously snapped on the overhead fluorescent lights.

Atjeh, the father.

Pensi with baby

shortly after birth; cutting and treating the umbilical cord; injecting both mother and offspring with preventive antibiotics; and then reuniting the two. No one could guarantee, however, that Pensi and Atjeh would again mate.

The National Zoo had formerly raised two wild-caught young orangutans, Susie and Butch. But when they reached sexual maturity they behaved as brother and sister and refused to mate. Only after they were separated and sent to different zoos did they successfully breed with other orangutans, thus pointing out the uncertainty of sexual compatibility between orangutans.

Pensi was specially recruited to be Atjeh's mate by General Curator Jaren G. Horsley and Mammal Curator Larry Collins because she had been born in captivity and reared by her mother. Since Atjeh had also been raised by his mother, it was thought that such a common experience would make it more likely that Pensi would rear her offspring. Horsley and Collins, believing it important to start producing second-generation young, traded a gorilla for Pensi.

The investment bore fruit once more when Atjeh and Pensi bred again several months after the death of Pensi's first-born. By May

of 1977 she was pregnant a second time.

Pensi's earlier pregnancy had been relatively trouble-free. This time, however, complications arose. Toward the middle of June, vaginal bleeding began. She also appeared to be having abdominal spasms or contractions.

Now the fear arose that she might abort her fetus. In an attempt to prevent a miscarriage, Zoo veterinarians prescribed the same female hormones used to maintain pregnancy in humans. They were spoon-fed to Pensi by Bond and the senior ape keeper, Walter Tucker, after being mixed with custard and applesauce, Pensi's favorite treats. After three days the bleeding stopped and the fetus seemed out of danger. Pensi's progress was monitored daily for the next six months by Bond and Tucker, both of whom still felt keenly the loss of the first baby.

The remainder of Pensi's pregnancy proved uneventful until December 14, 1977. That morning, Tucker left his home in Southeast Washington an hour early in his rush to get to the Zoo to see if Pensi had yet given birth. The day before, his sixth sense—cultivated during his 23 years as an animal keeper and 16 as an ape keeper—told him Pensi's second birth was near.

Had a different animal been pregnant, it might have been watched around the clock. But orangutans are sensitive, secretive creatures who enjoy solitude and privacy. Not wishing to upset the normal nighttime isolation of the apes from humans, the keepers had left Pensi alone at night.

Tucker's intuition that birth was imminent was reinforced by the Zoo's medical technologists, who had analyzed Pensi's urine with the Subhuman Primate Pregnancy Test Kit and tentatively forecast on December 13 that birth would occur within 48 hours.

At 5:30 a.m. Tucker's foresight was rewarded when he snapped on the overhead fluorescent lights. Pensi stirred. Then she picked up a moving bundle of reddish fur and ambled across the 12-by-12-foot cage in the uneven gait of orangutans. With both hands she held her newborn.

A burly six-footer with a salt-and-pepper mustache, Tucker has developed the trust of all the great apes in his charge. He always carries sticks of chewing gum and Life Savers in his shirt pocket to reward them. Such treats help keepers establish rapport and enable them to gain some control over the independent-minded animals. It was this relationship that prompted Pensi to amble toward him that morning with her new infant. He noticed that it was a male and that, again, Pensi had failed to sever the umbilical cord. Nevertheless, the sounds the baby made heartened him.

"It made you feel good," he remembers. "You can tell by the tone of the cry whether a baby ape is healthy. This one was only two or three hours old, and you could hear him crying in the basement. He obviously sported a good set of lungs."

Satisfied with the infant's appearance, Tucker set in motion the Zoo's plan to medically treat mother and offspring. He placed a phone call to Miles Roberts, curator in charge of the great apes. Mitchell Bush, the Zoo's chief veterinarian, was out of town, so Roberts called Suzanne Kennedy, an exotic-animal veterinarian who was then in her second year of internship at the National Zoo.

Kennedy quickly drove to the Zoo hospital where she met Jack Hoopes, another veterinary intern. By virtue of her seniority, Kennedy would be in charge. Hospital assistants, meanwhile, rapidly loaded the veterinarian's van with all the medical paraphernalia needed to immobilize Pensi and treat the infant. Equipment included a newly purchased incubator in which the newborn would be placed while Pensi recovered from the drug; surgical needles, bandage, restraint boxes, ointment, umbilical tape; an emergency kit; stimulants, oxygen, tracheal tubes (orangutans can suffocate under anesthesia and the tubes may be used to direct oxygen to the lungs); CI744, an anesthetic drug; and an electrocardiograph and defibrilator in case of a cardiac arrest.

Roberts, Melanie Bond and Walter Tucker distract Pensi while Dr. Kennedy injects the immobilizing drug.

Dr. Jack
Hoopes

"Anytime we perform a major immobilization, tremendous preparation takes place," says Kennedy. "We try to foresee any potential problem because we can't waste time going back to the hospital for some piece of equipment."

Despite almost two years of experience working with Zoo animals, Kennedy felt uneasy about immobilizing Pensi. She had never before been in charge of anesthetizing one of the great apes.

After arriving at the Small Mammal House, Kennedy decided to use a 4-foot aluminum pole with an attached hypodermic syringe to administer the immobilizing drug rather than shoot Pensi with a tranquilizing gun.

Using the pole syringe is not easy, for it must be maneuvered through the narrow, 6-inch-wide space between the thick steel bars. If Pensi sees it, she will agilely avoid it. All of the great apes at the Zoo recognize the veterinarians on sight, and react violently whenever they come close to their cages. However, once an orangutan or gorilla realizes it is not the object of the veterinarian's visit, it calms down. On this morning, however, something like pandemonium reigned. The great apes were already excited, having heard the newborn baby's squeals. Some had already started bouncing wildly across their cages, swinging and screaming. Keepers and vets grew conscious of the need to keep the apes from panicking any further.

The plan called for Tucker, Bond, and Roberts to remain in front of Pensi's cage to distract her. Meanwhile, Kennedy would ap-

proach from the side of the cage, carefully concealing the pole syringe from the sight of the other apes by holding it under her coat.

Tucker and Bond started feeding Pensi oranges while Kennedy prepared the pole syringe. Because Pensi now sat in the front of the cage, Kennedy realized she needed a 4-foot extension of the pole to reach her. As she started attaching it, she inadvertently banged the wall behind Pensi's cage. While she had not seen Kennedy, the orangutan knew someone was behind her, and started casting nervous glances over her shoulder.

Kennedy had decided on a dose of 150 milligrams of CI744. It is considered one of the best anesthetic drugs to immobilize the great apes because it is metabolized quickly, enabling the ape to recover rapidly and minimizing the danger of suffocation.

"We had given her 175 milligrams 10 months earlier, and while she didn't go under well, we could handle her," recalled Kennedy. The dose had to be lighter this time because it was uncertain how much energy the birth had taken out of Pensi.

The trio at the front of the cage succeeded in keeping Pensi occupied, at the same time banging their keys on the bars to camouflage the noise being made by Kennedy as she slipped the pole syringe between the bars. When he saw the pole coming closer, Roberts distracted Pensi further by reaching inside the cage. As she took a swipe at his arm, Kennedy jammed the pole syringe into her hindquarter. The orangutan rolled over, looked at Kennedy, and then rolled back into a sitting position, the infant still clutching its mother's neck. After a short time passed, it was clear the dose had been inadequate.

Kennedy supplemented the first dose with 35 milligrams more. Because Pensi was now slightly sluggish, the second injection was more easily administered. Still Pensi did not go down. Nor did anyone dare attempt to go into the cage and take the baby.

Maddeningly, even a second small supplement proved too little. With growing apprehension, Kennedy increased the dosage and, after waiting 10 minutes, injected Pensi again. "She was almost there but it still wasn't enough," remembers Kennedy, by now seriously worried. After another 10 minutes, she injected an additional 35 milligrams. This would have to be the last dose.

During the previous two injections, Pensi had started nibbling on the baby's right foot, finally biting a nail off one toe. Bond, who

14

considers orangutans her favorite animal, had seen them tranquilized before. "You never know how any drug will affect them," she says. "They may do strange things."

The last injection had done the trick. At 10:52 a.m. Pensi slumped to the floor of her cage. Roberts, who like Kennedy wore a surgical cap, mask, and gloves, stole into the cage and took the baby, placing it immediately in the incubator.

Meanwhile, William Peratino, a weight lifter and the hospital's resident animal keeper, entered the cage and propped Pensi in a sitting position against the bars. On the outside of the cage, Roberts and Dr. Hoopes each grabbed an arm while Kennedy gave Pensi a pre-prepared injection of iron dextran to help her development of red blood cells (she borders on being anemic), a hormone to control any postpartum bleeding and to stimulate lactation, and Flocillin, a long-acting penicillin to control infections. Then Kennedy examined the baby, which weighed almost 5 pounds and appeared to be in good condition. She tied off the umbilical cord with iodine-soaked tape, severed the cord, and sutured the stump. The baby, like the mother, was then given a shot of iron dextran and Flocillin, a blood sample was taken, and the toe treated with antiseptic.

At 11:15 a.m.—22 minutes after Pensi's last dosage—humans vacated the cage. The baby, meanwhile, remained in the incubator, within sight of Pensi. Around one o'clock, the mother orangutan began focusing her attention on her offspring, still lying in the strange contraption.

At this point, keeper Bond, also wearing the protective surgical mask, cap, and gloves, removed the baby from the incubator and placed it in an adjoining, hay-filled cage. Pensi watched intently through a small hole in the metal door separating the two cages.

Another tense moment loomed. Would Pensi take the offspring back, or would she reject it? The Zoo staff involved were unaware if other zoos had ever forcibly removed an orangutan infant from its mother before, and then tried to reunite them. Who knew what subtle factors operated?

When the door between the cages finally opened, Pensi moved at once. She walked to her son, examined him carefully, smelled him, then picked him up. The human observers breathed a heavy sigh of relief.

But life at a zoo presents one crisis after another. Now, as with Pensi's first baby, the crucial question became whether normal nursing would be reinstituted.

With the discovery that the young orangutan had been nursing, another major worry disappeared. If an orangutan infant fails to nurse properly, it can dehydrate within a few days and die. In other zoos, baby orangutans have been removed from their parents when they are only two or three days old because of uncertainty as to whether nursing has taken place. In such cases, the orangutans are subsequently raised by humans.

But as Pensi and her baby did well once reunited, the Zoo decided to leave the line of ape cages open to the public. At that time it was winter, and the relatively few visitors made it less likely that Pensi would become upset by crowds. The Zoo's graphics department hastily put up a sign giving the date of birth and the names of the parents.

Atjeh, the male parent, viewed his progeny through a peephole in his metal cage door. There were fears he might become dangerously jealous of Pensi's attention to the baby were he allowed in the same cage.

During the first week, Pensi behaved as expected, and the infant gained strength. Meanwhile, Zoo employees concocted far-fetched reasons to leave their offices and walk over to the Small Mammal House to see the infant. Others packed their lunches and ate them in front of Pensi's cage.

The only nagging concern—and it seemed minor—was the baby's toe, which soon swelled to twice its normal size. Still, the veterinarians didn't feel it was serious enough to re-

Dr. Suzanne Kennedy

15

Dr. Mitchell Bush, veterinarian.

move the baby from Pensi for treatment. But two days before Christmas, Bond noticed a white growth forming in the young orangutan's mouth. Possibly in an effort to heal it, Pensi picked at the white stuff. Bond reported the condition, but immediate concern seemed unwarranted as the baby continued to nurse normally. The white formation continued to grow, however, and the day after Christmas, Tucker noticed that the infant's lower lip had become limp and bloody, so distorting the mouth that the baby could no longer suckle.

No choice then remained but to remove the infant from Pensi, which meant that the orangutan baby, if cured, would have to be hand reared by humans. The medical treatment would take so long that Pensi would stop producing milk and no longer be able to nurse her son, a process that can last up to two or three years.

Bush called several physicians for their opinions about the young orangutan, surprisingly similar in body structure to a human baby. Gordon W. Daisley, Jr., a pediatrician, suggested that the infection might be thrush, a potentially fatal fungal infection also found in human babies.

This time the immobilization of Pensi turned out to be quick and easy. After one poke, Pensi climbed up on the shelf in her cage and passed out. The keepers carefully removed the baby from its mother's inert form and lowered Pensi onto the cage floor, lest she fall from the shelf on awaking.

Bush labeled the infant's condition critical.

"I looked in its mouth and saw considerable tissue damage. The odor was overwhelming," says Bush, shaking his head.

The infant would have to be kept in the incubator and watched around the clock. Bond was chosen to become the baby's surrogate mother, a role that required feeding him formula from a baby bottle every two hours, picking him up and comforting him when he cried, and cleaning up after him.

Four months earlier, the old library in the hospital building had been converted into offices for Hoopes and Kennedy. These offices now became a nursery for the ailing young orangutan and a temporary home for Bond.

Rushing to her apartment to stock up for the next few days, Bond grabbed canned soup, TV dinners, and T-shirts, and asked her roommate to take care of her 26 various pets.

Meanwhile, technicians at the Zoo hospital analyzed the baby's blood and urine. An infected piece of tissue from the baby's mouth was placed in a nutrient culture to determine the type of bacteria present. Simultaneously, another culture was grown to see what types of antibiotics would work best against the infection. The baby had a mixed bacterial infection, including staphylococcus, streptococcus, and *Escherichia coli;* but a fungus did not grow in a culture, leaving the diagnosis of thrush unverified.

In analyzing the cultures and the blood and urine taken from the infant, Betsy Smith, the Zoo's chief medical technologist, contributed information that was vital to evaluating the infant's condition and monitoring the various treatment schedules on the infant's functions. Throughout the course of the baby orangutan's treatment, the clinician visited the laboratory to obtain the latest set of data which would help them evaluate its progress.

Two broad-spectrum antibiotics were administered to the infant, an anti-fungal liquid placed in its mouth, and an iodine-based antiseptic swabbed on both mouth and toe. A formula of soybean milk and dextrose became its daily diet. Liquid amino acids and B-complex vitamins were injected under the skin for slow absorption into the system. In the 12 days since birth, the infant had lost 200 grams, or almost half a pound of weight—not a good sign.

After the veterinarians left for the night, Bond curled up on a piece of foam rubber and covered herself with her coat. "I was afraid to go to sleep because I might not hear him cry," says Bond. "I found out later that was a joke. You tune in on his sounds so quickly and automatically."

On the second night Bond used a sleeping bag, and on the third night a Monkey House keeper lent her a canvas cot. Bond remembers trying to think like an orangutan mother. When the infant started crying during the second night, Bond took it out of the incubator and slept on her back; the little orangutan slept comfortably on her chest.

"He rested better that way and it seemed more natural," says Bond, nevertheless determined not to treat the infant like a human.

"I was opposed to, and to some extent instructed to avoid, making a little person out of him, with diapers and baby clothes," she recalls. Whenever she held him, she simply wrapped the infant loosely in a towel.

"He was not a person, and would have to grow up like an orangutan. If he made it, it would be easier for him in the long run if we didn't make it harder to adjust to being an orangutan," she reflects.

Every morning one of the Zoo's three practicing veterinarians checked on the infant. Every night Bond called Bush at home to report on the infant's temperature and condition. The baby's urine was checked daily to make sure he was well hydrated and passing liquids properly. Blood samples were scheduled for every two days, and the baby's diet was supplemented with *Lactobacillus*, a lactic acid-forming bacteria used in helping digestion. The antibiotics being administered

to him suppressed these "good" bacteria.

On the third day, Bond began to show the strain of her 24-hour vigils broken only with cat naps. Roberts recruited three other female keepers to work alternating 24-hour shifts.

On December 30, four days after being taken from its mother, the orangutan took a turn for the worse. "I thought he was fading on us," said Bush, who quickly switched to two new antibiotics despite a calculated risk that one of them could cause kidney damage. But both Bush and Dr. Daisley, who stopped almost daily at the Zoo hospital to check on the primate patient, felt something had to be

Azy took a turn for the worse, and the decision was made to operate.

Melanie Bond, surrogate mother for baby Azy.

done. The mouth was simply not healing.

The next few days proved uneventful, although the baby continually ran a fever over 100 degrees F and normal temperature for orangutans, as for humans, is 98.6 degrees.

As the doctors struggled with the medical problems, the keepers coped handily as surrogate orangutan mothers. Linda Mahn, a Monkey House keeper, and Carol Partington and Pat Larkin, both keepers in the Small Mammal House, joined the ranks of the baby's substitute mothers.

Because the baby's survival as a second-generation orangutan would signify an important zoological achievement, an informal network sprang up at the Zoo with the keeper-mothers grilled daily about the infant's progress.

But the network began humming ominously on January 6, when swelling appeared in the upper portion of the infant's left leg. Then, on January 8, the right elbow seemed inflamed. The next day granular cysts, or dead kidney cells, showed up in the baby's urine, immediately spreading fear that the new antibiotic had not only failed to heal the mouth infection but also might now be damaging the kidneys.

Although the antibiotics may actually have been causing the kidneys to work overtime and thus slough off dead cells, a concerned Mitch Bush again consulted Daisley and other physicians.

Bush decided to switch to the fifth antibiotic in 15 days. Like the previous drug, it also had potentially dangerous side effects. In humans it is associated with bone-marrow depression—the failure of the marrow to produce red and white blood cells—and can lead to death from lack of white cells. The baby was already known to have a low blood count bordering on anemia.

The next day the right elbow and left hip remained swollen. Bush decided to operate on the 11th. He opened the elbow, drained it, and flushed it with saline and a local antiseptic, afterward ordering hot packs to be administered to try to draw out the pus.

Though the baby's mouth began to heal—a good sign—the elbow and hip both remained badly infected. Bush was especially worried about the elbow because if the baby lost use of the arm, it would severely limit his ability to swing in his cage.

On January 16, only five days after the first operation, Bush decided to again open the elbow and to open the hip for the first time. One of the physicians Bush had consulted, Douglas McKay, Chief of the Department of Orthopedic Surgery at Children's Hospital, volunteered to do the operation since he had performed similar ones on human babies.

Reminiscent of a hospital's general operating room, the Zoo's operating room is smaller, but equipped with everything necessary to perform operations ranging from neurological to orthopedic to cardiovascular. Dr. McKay would have at his finger tips anesthetic and emergency resuscitation equipment (including a cardiac defibrilator), an electrocautery unit, an EKG monitor for the heartbeat, and a suction machine to help clean the infection out of the orangutan's joints.

Shortly before the operation began, the Indonesian Embassy named the baby "Azy," a combination of his parents' names. The embassy names all the Zoo's orangutans, as Indonesia encompasses the species' homeland.

It took an hour and a half to open the elbow and hip joints, flush them out using the suction machine, and put in drains to let the pus flow out. What pleased everybody was that Azy's joints appeared undamaged.

The next day Daisley admitted that "If Azy had been a human baby, he would be on his way to heaven by now."

While the operation appeared to be a success, Azy's left leg and right elbow remained swollen. On January 18, Bush operated again, taking the drains out of the hip and elbow and packing the hip joint with antiseptic-soaked gauze.

The next day everything started going

18

wrong. Azy's temperature peaked at 104.6 degrees F, and the prognosis wasn't good. Even Bush's optimism was fading, for Azy had been on the new antibiotic for nine days "and we really hadn't gotten on top of the infection in the joints. My main concern was that while we might be able to save him, he would end up with two crippled joints. They had been infected so long they could develop a really bad secondary joint disease."

A sixth antibiotic was prescribed. Hoopes felt that this was "the last big gun. If he didn't rally now, he would probably die."

Even on this critical day with his blistering temperature, Azy still had his appetite going for him. Despite all the injections and three operations, he had gained a full pound since being taken from his mother.

On January 21 Bush operated for the fourth time, opening the elbow joint one last time. He also prescribed paregoric to slow down Azy's gastrointestinal system and allow the new antibiotic more time to be absorbed. Late that evening, Azy's temperature broke, returning to normal and even dipping at one point to 96.5 degrees F.

By January 22 the drama was over. While Azy remained under the veterinarians' care and had 24-hour keeper-mothers for another 18 days, he was out of danger. Zoo Director Theodore Reed, who was the Zoo veterinarian prior to 1958, praised his staff's teamwork. "Twenty years ago, believe me," he added, "Azy wouldn't have pulled through. We didn't have the knowledge or the drugs."

From the moment Azy left his mother, Miles Roberts had been seeking a place to raise him, preferably with another orangutan of similar age. Bush learned that John Moore, director of the Rio Grande zoo in Albuquerque, New Mexico, and his wife were raising Bonnie, a one-year-old female. It was decided to send Azy there. Although he would be raised by humans, he would have another orangutan for a playmate.

On February 28, 1978, aboard a regular TWA flight to New Mexico, Bush and his wife, Lena May, took Azy to his new home. Bonnie and Azy—who one day may become mates—will return to the National Zoo after completion of a new $3 million ape house with 17-foot-high ceilings and huge outdoor yards designed to create a more natural environment and increase the possibility of more captive orangutan births. □

Seven-week-old Azy on a flight to the Rio Grande Zoo in Albuquerque, N.M.

SECTION I
DENIZENS

THE EXOTIC COMMUNITY

ECOLOGY OF A ZOO

Theodore H. Reed
Director, National Zoological Park

The trials of Pensi and Azy illustrate the complexities of a modern zoological garden: the interacting concerns of the animal keepers, curators, mechanics, veterinarians, and administrative staff. For a few days, all their thoughts and actions centered on Azy, this one little ball of an orangutan.

Being nestled in the valley of Rock Creek, about three miles from the White House, we feel like residents of a miniature city within a city. But if, at heart, we are an exotic city, at the same time we are a mundane one. We wrestle with the same problems any city faces: water supply, sewage, electrical systems, telephones, and security. We constantly worry about fire, and the flooding of Rock Creek. We are concerned with snow removal, garbage disposal, and even parking problems. We are prone to the vagaries of high winds knocking down trees, imperiling visitors as well as our animal residents, even perhaps allowing their escape. Once just such a wind brought down a large tree limb onto one of the bear pits. After his initial shock, the bear investigated and decided to walk out. Fortunately, an alert Zoo policeman stood nearby. As the bear started clambering across the tree, the officer stood like Horatio at the bridge, coaxing the animal back with another limb until help arrived.

Like any small city we have different departments. We are accountable to a federal audit department ever vigilant that we live within our budget. We have an education department to provide information to visitors. Other staff members worry about the acquisition of food for residents and its storage and distribution.

Like any small community we have our "freeloaders"—the foxes, raccoons, opossums, chipmunks, and squirrels that come in from the surrounding woods and live among us. The raccoons and opossums seem to enjoy our numerous trash cans. The chipmunks and squirrels like to cadge food off the visitors and, before we instituted a "No Feeding" program, stole peanuts from the bears. It was always amusing to watch a cheeky little squirrel sneak in and grab a peanut almost from under the paws of a bear. Occasionally the raccoons and opossums raid the waterfowl ponds or pheasant runs. Then we have to step in, for it always seems that the raccoons select the most expensive birds, leaving the common mallards alone.

Our city's major purpose is to please, entertain, and educate the human visitor. The

Children play on one of the large-scale concrete-and-aggregate signs placed at the two main entrances to the Zoo's grounds.

Wading into the water is one of the many offspring of Joe Smith and Arusha, a breeding pair of Nile hippos who have produced 16 calves since being placed together in 1956.

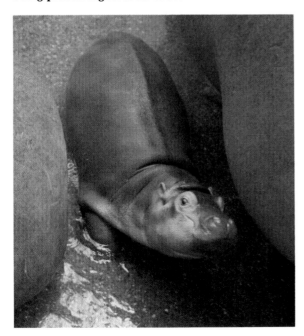

output of our industry, our product, is animals that have been successfully bred and raised, and the research and management papers that are dispersed throughout the world and used in other zoos, national parks, and universities. Another product we turn out is trained workers and scholars ready to assume positions in other zoos around the country.

To further illustrate the way in which we all interact, let us break down the Zoo into its simplest component: "The Exhibit."

The exhibit is the basic building block, the lowest common denominator of any zoological park. It encompasses all the problems, joys, and tragedies that any zoo may have. The five basic components of the exhibit are the animal, first; then the cage, the keeper, the label, and, finally, the visitor.

"The animal" may be anything from a polliwog to an elephant. About the smallest things I have ever seen exhibited were the first stages in the life of a jellyfish in a rather nice microscopic exhibit at a Japanese zoo. Generally speaking, the term "animal" includes more than an individual organism. It includes as well the social structure of the particular species: a pair of animals if it is a monogamous group, a herd or flock if that is appropriate.

The animals, of course, are selected for exhibition in a definite fashion. They are judged on their scientific interest, their rarity,

Veteran animal keeper Leroy Robertson, above, who worked at the Zoo for almost 30 years, shepherds Michael-John, the oldest giraffe in the Zoo's herd, indoors. Michael-John has sired all the giraffes born at the Zoo in recent years. Thomas Gray, top center, a carpenter, and Bess Frank, a keeper in the Zoo's new Beaver Valley exhibit, perform some of the everyday tasks that keep the Zoo running smoothly.

their potential for breeding, the possibility of their extinction, the ability of the Zoo to house, manage, and feed them, and on their appeal to the public. Some animals, such as the common prairie dog, are not highly endangered or of great scientific interest, yet they are tremendously popular with visitors. Then there are obligatory species. A major zoo is simply expected to have an elephant, a giraffe, a large snake, crocodiles, great apes, and certain monkeys and bears. Such stars of the show as the giant pandas draw in visitors who then find there are other animals—the acouchi or hyenas—that are extremely interesting and enjoyable to watch.

Certain animals are selected primarily for their scientific interest. For instance, we have maned wolves from South America at our Conservation and Research Center at Front Royal. A terrifically interesting animal from the scientific standpoint, the maned wolf exhibits certain solitary characteristics not found very often in canines. This is one reason why we think it will make a worthy exhibit one day.

The second component, the cage, can mean anything from a two-gallon fish bowl to something the size of Yellowstone National Park. It might be a 35-acre paddock such as we have for our Père David's deer, or one-third of an acre for our tigers. Some people have said that the giant pandas live in too large, or glorious, a house. My contention is that while they do have a better house than the Director, I have not had millions of visitors tromping through my front room.

Although the cage, whatever its size, is a confinement area, it contains all the things an animal should need: an area for sleep; an area in which to hide; and trees or something equivalent to climb. If it is a swimming animal, its cage will include a pool; if not, some source of water. I once defined the attributes of a proper cage as meeting the physical and psychological needs of the animal while securely confining it in a manner aesthetically pleasing to the public. The idea, of course, is to get the animal's cage to look as unlike a cage as possible.

"Iron bars do not a prison make," the poet Sheridan said, but they do look just like a prison. If we can create the illusion of freedom through the use of moats and stonework and still maintain the animals in their confined areas, both the public and the animals will be content. Moats are not infallible barriers, however, for they can freeze up. In one Midwestern zoo the moat froze over and filled up with snow. As a result, the polar bears walked out. At the Buffalo zoo a few years ago, snow drifted so high over the fence that the reindeer walked over the top and wandered all over the park.

Though we try to provide a natural environment with grass and trees, it is a constant problem keeping plants alive in a relatively small area where animals live all year round. On the plains of Africa, giraffes can nibble on the abundant acacia trees growing there. While the animals trim the trees to a certain height, they normally don't destroy them. In the Zoo, however, we have to protect the native trees we have, otherwise the giraffes would eat every leaf and chew off every shred of bark. And though we would prefer to have our animals live on a grassy terrain, it is almost impossible. Either they eat the grass or wear it down to dirt. For these as well as for sanitary reasons, we often have no choice but to put them on cement. Yet I've seen many changes for the better in the past few years: more air conditioning, temperature and humidity control, and use of safety glass make the exhibits both more aesthetically pleasing and also benefit the animals.

The third component, the keeper, includes all of us who support and care for the captive animal. The importance of the keeper, who brings the animal its food and notes its state of health, and the curator, who studies the species, is so great that a chapter of this book is devoted to their work. But it also includes the maintenance crew who unplug the drains, replace the wires, pour the cement and sweep the grounds; the gardeners who trim the trees and bring in branches for the animals to eat; the farm crew at Front Royal who grow alfalfa and hay; the police who

maintain order; the veterinarians who handle exotic animals with toothaches, births, and stomachaches; and pathologists, who help the animals that are living by studying animals that have died.

Although I consider the keeper the basic building block, all of us who work at the Zoo are oriented toward the same goal. We are shepherds of different talents.

The fourth component, the label, is the broad term for any educational information. The cage label should include the scientific name, the range, the age of the animals, and details on the individual animal within; it can go on at great length and provide a great deal of zoological information about the animal. Under the broad term "label" could come the entire educational program: the docents, the lecturers, the movies, guided tours, even the directional signs.

William Mann, my immediate predecessor, spoke with me one time about labels and signs. After 26 years in his profession, he was considered one of the "grand old men." Bill instructed me that every cage should have a proper label because when a visitor came to the Zoo he would find at least one animal that piqued his interest sufficiently to make him want to learn more about it. The visitor may walk by a thousand animals and not read a single label, Bill said. Then he comes to the thousand-and-first and wants to know all about that weird and wonderful creature.

Prior to my becoming director I had toured the Zoo with Dr. Mann many times. He would pass by the kookaburra cage and glance at this bird, whose raucous, braying call is reminiscent of that of a jackass. "Twenty-six years on exhibition," he would say proudly. "Pretty good record for a kookaburra." After he retired, I once found myself showing some visitors around. At the kookaburra cage I said in my most pontifical tone, "Twenty-seven years on exhibition. Pretty good for a kookaburra." Later on, the elder keeper in the Bird House stopped by, apparently delegated to speak. "Young man," he said, "since you're just starting out, maybe you should know that at least three kookaburras have been exhibited underneath that sign." No one had ever had the courage to tell Dr. Mann.

Another time, I found a blue sheep which, according to the label, was unbelievably old. When I questioned the keepers about the animal's apparent youth and friskiness, I found out that the label had originally been posted when the sheep's parents had come in as young lambs many years before. So it's a constant process—reviewing and checking labels to keep them current.

The fifth component is the visitor—*Homo sapiens*, with all his curiosity and his love of animals, and sometimes with his deep misunderstanding and ignorance. In one way he is our major reason for being, for without him there would probably be no National Zoological Park. We might be a research center or primarily a conservation and breeding farm, but we would not be the public zoo that was mandated in 1890 by an Act of Congress.

The reasons visitors come are many. For some it's an educational experience, for others simply a way to while away an idle afternoon. Some people come specifically to see the giant pandas or their favorite ape. Frequently, when the news media has announced the birth of a giraffe or a new acquisition, local residents will stop by just to see that animal.

We have studied our visitors from time to time, wondering how attentive they are to our labels, how effectively we've presented information. While most of them have a genuine love and concern for the animals, some unfortunately lack understanding of wild animals: they want to pet them; they want to feed them. We try to prohibit this because we know that we are feeding our residents a nutritious, well-balanced diet. Then, of course, there is that very small minority which takes a strange pleasure in harassing or teasing the animals. We must protect the visitor from himself, and that is why we have visitor fences, prohibition signs, police, and keepers on public patrol duty. Surprisingly, we spend probably somewhere between 75 and 80 percent of our time and effort managing *people* rather than animals.

On the other hand, while we expend great effort on making our cages aesthetically pleasing to the visitor, the animal is, of course, the central factor. For example, in the present Monkey House, we felt we could not duplicate trees from the various parts of the world in which the monkeys are native. Even at great expense the most sturdy fake tree would not withstand the wear and tear of monkey play. Because such trees would still look like fakes, we installed fiber-glass play material, making a kind of jungle gym. Each exhibit is properly designed for the activity patterns of the animals, be they leapers, swingers, or climbers. The jungle gym allows

the animal to exhibit its natural and special talents of motion and activity. Although I've had some complaints that it looks much too artificial, the animals seem to be perfectly happy with it. Personally, I feel that it displays the animal better than the fake trees would have, and that we are in the business of displaying animals, not demonstrating how clever we are at simulating trees.

The world of zoos, like everything else on this planet, has been evolving, changing, and growing. I can remember sitting on a guardrail in the old days with the Portland, Oregon, zoo Director Jack Marks, looking at a lion. We knew he wasn't eating and he wasn't very active; he obviously didn't feel well. But I couldn't get my hands on him, let alone take his temperature or get a blood sample. If he looked like he had a headache, we gave him aspirin. If he looked like he was having a digestive upset, we tried to medicate him. In those early days animals often received minimal treatment because the mere act of catching and treating the animal would incur more dangers. Today, with the development of "capture guns" and "flying syringes," it is possible to immobilize animals like Pensi and use advanced techniques that constantly amaze me. When I compare how I first had to practice veterinary medicine with the techniques our vet staff now use, I feel as though I had been practicing witchcraft back then.

Certainly our modern concept of what a zoo is and what it should be doing is different than that of the ancient "gardens of intelligence" in China, the Hanging Gardens of Babylon, or the menagerie of Queen Hatshepsut in the 18th dynasty of Egypt. The oldest modern zoo is that in the Schönbrunn Palace in Vienna, Austria, founded by Queen Maria Teresa in 1752. The guiding concepts of zoos these days are their dedication to education, scientific investigations of the animals, conservation, and breeding. This is far different from the menagerie which consisted of groups of odd and interesting animals from faraway places assembled for the amusement and wonderment of the elite.

The National Zoo was founded with the intention of being different from the standard menagerie of the 1890s. It was given the noble mandate for the "advancement of science, education and recreation for the people" and was made a part of the Smithsonian Institution, which has as its mission "the increase and diffusion of knowledge

among men." Although the Zoo's original purpose was to undertake breeding demonstrations and to become a place of scientific study and inquiry at the nation's capital, these thoughts were almost too advanced at the time. Because of our financial support structure and the immense and immediate popularity of the Zoo with the citizens of Washington, we became instead a more standard zoo. Still, there has always been the thought and belief that, as "the National Zoo," we were a little different and a little special. Our mission is, and has always been, to take leadership in areas of animal management, breeding, and research. Because of external factors, our concepts of how this leadership should be taken and what we should do have changed since the Zoo's beginning. The fluctuations in the conditions of animals throughout the world also necessitated modifications in our thinking and our management plans. In the early days we were not as concerned with breeding the animals into multiple generations as we are now.

Our concept of the animals as a sacred trust for generations of man and animals yet unborn is relatively new, forced upon us by the threat of extinction of many animals. Certainly when the Zoo was founded in 1890, and at the beginning of the American zoo movement, which took place a few years earlier, we did not believe that the great abundance and diversity of exotic wildlife from Africa, Asia, and South America would be threatened with annihilation. Even within my own tenure in the zoo world, about 28 years, there have been serious changes in zoo thinking. I recall some of the older zoo people claiming that "for some species of animals the zoos will be the last hope." Now, you hear the statement, "For many species of animals the zoos will be the *only* hope." It is unnerving and terrifying to see what has happened to the populations of wild animals worldwide within the past 20 years. Perhaps even the idea that we will be helpful in saving some animals from extinction is a forlorn hope. It is debatable whether our breeding programs, coupled with the scientific investigations necessary to support these programs, are more important than the educational programs the zoos can offer in the urban centers where they are located. Can we really be a major instrument of educational influence to the general public and so help save the animals? Unfortunately, we will not answer that question for 50 or 100 years.

Speaking of the future, one can expect that there will be more zoos with smaller collections and with more intense studies of their animals. More breeding, more educational work, and certainly more cooperation in exchanging of animals can be expected. We zoos will not consider our animals as our own parochial creatures, but rather as a trust for the national or even international species pool. We will stop talking about how our particular animals are doing, but will speak of how giraffes, gorillas, or okapis are doing on a worldwide basis.

"The Zoo" is a weird, wonderful, exciting, frustrating, glorious, rewarding, disheartening, beautiful place to work. We who are privileged to be a part of zoos, to associate with the animals and involve ourselves in the thrilling activities, explorations, and research of the Zoo, are indeed a special brand of people. The Welsh have a beautiful poem that states, "How fortunate is the man who has found his love while he is young." We who are on the so-called staff of the Zoo are indeed fortunate to have found our love.

Let there be no mistake about who is running the Zoo. I am, as director, privileged to sign the papers, plead for the money, run, direct, and care for the Zoo. But the animals are really the directors. I am only the chief caretaker for them. The animals give the orders. I often wonder, "Who then *is* the director?" I have come to the conclusion that it is Atjeh, father of little Azy. He is the thinking one; he is the one that can plan; he has the devious mind to make us humans dance to his tune. I often think he is sitting there contemplating what he is going to have us do next. Somehow he gets the word out to all the other animals as to what shall be done. How they shall make us humans behave ourselves. What we shall do for them.

He is the boss. □

Tomoka, opposite top, a lowland gorilla, was only the second gorilla born in captivity in America. At top left, youngster examines a Galapagos turtle in its warm-weather pen, while a young panda buff, left center, watches Ling-Ling in her outdoor yard. One of the giraffes' more familiar sights, left, is that of crowds of people, now raised to the animals' eye level by a new concrete viewing ramp.

29

THE EARLY YEARS

EVOLUTION OF THE ZOO

Thomas Crosby and Kathleen A. Lynch

Dunk and Gold-Dust, two unruly elephants from the Adam Forepaugh Show, journeyed through downtown Washington, D.C., on the afternoon of April 30, 1891, en route to their new home at the National Zoological Park. Beside the pair rode Patsy Meagher, Forepaugh's elephant keeper, mounted on a prancing cream-colored circus horse.

Leading the parade, also on horseback, were the Zoo's Head Keeper William H. Blackburne, former master animal trainer with the Barnum & Bailey Circus; Acting Zoo Director Frank Baker; other dignitaries; and the *Washington Star* reporter covering this symbolic opening of the Zoo. Upon reaching Rock Creek on the city's outskirts, the elephants cavorted in the water and stood, the *Star* reported, "... knee deep ... drinking deep draughts and squirting streams over themselves. ..." "All the small boys in Washington who were not at the circus that day" followed the procession, recounted William M. Mann, who, as Zoo director 34 years later, was to inherit problems already germinating on that clear spring day.

The National Zoological Park, the world's 49th zoo, was the first to be dedicated to the preservation of native species. Like the White House and the Capitol, the Zoo's grounds and all its inhabitants belonged to the American people. The U.S. Congress, however, refused in this case to assume its traditional responsibility for preserving the national heritage, and therefore, until 1971, the District of Columbia had to share the Zoo's operating expenses. This peculiar arrangement, stemming in part from a running conflict over the Zoo's raison d'être, provoked competition with city agencies for funding. This in turn slowed the Zoo's growth into a center for conservation, research, and education. At times, its very survival looked doubtful.

From the beginning, management of the Zoo rested with the Smithsonian Institution, founded in 1846 from a bequest by the Englishman James Smithson. The Smithsonian's Department of Living Animals formed the nucleus of the Zoo's original collection, and Smithsonian money fed the animals during the winter of 1892, the Zoo's first deficit-budget year. Perhaps even more important, it was Smithsonian leadership that kept alive the dream of a national zoological park "for the advancement of science and the instruction and recreation of the people."

William T. Hornaday—hunter, naturalist, author, one of America's earliest conser-

William H. Blackburne, the Zoo's first head
keeper, shows off Dunk and Gold-Dust, top, the
Zoo's first permanent residents. Bottom,
Blackburne, right, visits Jumbina, the Zoo's tallest
and "meanest ever" African elephant.

vationists, and chief taxidermist of the Smithsonian National Museum—had first envisioned a national zoo. In 1887, a year after an unsuccessful attempt to replenish the Museum's stuffed bison exhibit, Smithsonian Secretary Spencer F. Baird dispatched Hornaday to secure fresh skins "before it should become too late." After months combing the Montana plains, once the range of five million bison, the expedition netted a collection that included 24 skins, 16 complete skeletons, 51 dry skulls, and two yearling calves. "In view of the almost complete extinction of the species, we may fairly consider [these specimens] of almost priceless value," wrote Baird in the Smithsonian's annual report for 1887.

After Baird's death, Hornaday sought and gained a powerful ally for his cause in Baird's successor, astrophysicist Samuel Pierpont Langley. Langley inherited a Smithsonian with animals overflowing its grounds. Some of the beasts were sent to the U.S. Insane Asylum (now St. Elizabeths Hospital) where they provided harmless diversion for patients. Others took up residence at the Philadelphia zoo after taxidermists and scientists had finished studying them. The new Secretary created and put Hornaday in charge of the Institution's first Department of Living Animals, 220 specimens including two American bison, turtles, snakes, hares, foxes, squirrels, raccoons, and a monkey. These animals, wrote Langley, were "crowded together in one small, ill-ventilated building heated by steam, which during exhibition hours is usually filled with visitors to an uncomfortable extent."

Hornaday continued to lobby for the creation of a national zoo, and popular interest in the idea began to grow. Finally, so that "these animals might not be only for the subject of study, but be expected to increase as they do not in ordinary captivity," Senator James Burnie Beck of Kentucky introduced a bill for the Zoo's creation on April 23, 1888. In Langley's words, "the buffalo, the mountain sheep and goat, the elk, and other vanishing races of the continent deserve protection at the hands of the Government."

The proposal won almost universal approv-

A class observes the bison, newly transferred from the Mall to the Zoo's Rock Creek site. Simple fencing illustrates inexperience in ensuring the safety of animals and of the public.

al in the press. The *San Francisco Call,* for instance, spoke of the growing scarcity of animals once plentiful in America: "... if nothing is done to preserve them, in a few years they will have disappeared as completely as the pterodactyl." But the bill was attached to the federal sundry appropriations bill and was not passed by Congress.

In the meantime, under Langley's direction, Hornaday inspected land in the valley of Rock Creek, where a 167-acre tract would eventually become the site of the Zoo.

A similar zoo proposal was introduced at the next session of Congress. This time it was attached to the District of Columbia appropriations bill, the annual authorization to the U.S. Treasury to provide the federal city with half the money it needed. The draft legislation estimated the probable cost of the Rock Creek site at $200,000. A bargain even in the 1890s, the land's hilly topography made it less than appealing to commercial developers, but ideal for a zoo. "Here, not only the wild goat, the mountain sheep and their congeners would find the rocky cliffs which are their natural home," Langley argued in favor of the site, "but the beavers brooks in which to breed and replenish their dying race, aquatic birds and beasts their natural home."

The proposal met with a hospitable reception in the Senate, whose members appreciated the need for a national, scientifically oriented zoo, dedicated to saving animals from extinction and offering naturalists and zoologists a place to study animals at close range. The Congress itself had set a precedent for preserving wildlife as early as 1871, when it created Yellowstone National Park.

The House, however, reacted more parochially, mirroring the general public's reluctance to view wildlife as a natural resource. At that time, America's half-dozen zoos, scarcely more than menageries, featured lions, zebras, and other exotics to attract visitors. Illustrating the widespread apathy toward animal conservation and research, one politician objected to spending money to "have the Nebraska elk and the Florida alligator cooped up." Another congressman fancied animals he could not see at home, whereas isolationists asserted that spending money to import "foreign" species offended the spirit of the Constitution. Nevertheless, the parliamentary maneuver of appending the National Zoo proposal to the vital D.C. appropriations bill succeeded, and the bill passed and became law on March 2, 1889.

Leaving little doubt as to the antagonist in this drama, an 1891 political cartoon from the *Washington Post* depicts some of the sentiment aroused by Congress' refusal to appropriate all the funds needed to cover the Zoo's operating costs. Instead, the zoo proposal was appended to the D.C. appropriations bill, which drained the District coffers and thwarted the Zoo's goals of conservation and research.

As a creature of the D.C. appropriations bill, the Zoo was subject to the same financial conditions as the bill's other provisions: the federal government would pay half the expenses, the District the other half. The *Star* spoke for many critics of this arrangement:

"The foolishness and injustice of forcing the District into an unsolicited partnership with Uncle Sam in respect to the zoological park will become painfully clearer every time expenditure of money upon the project and the purposes for which the land is to be used come up for discussion ... If the District is to pay for the park as a local institution it wants something to say concerning its management, it wants the entire space thrown open to public use and enjoyment, with none of it reserved for the purely scientific purposes of the government ..."

This unprecedented division of expenses between federal and local government drew up battle lines for a long argument over whether the Zoo's purpose was to promote recreation or conservation.

Another year went by before Congress authorized its share of the money to manage the Zoo. For fiscal year 1891, Congress finally appropriated $92,000 to cover all expenses, including new access roads and sewers, and $2,000 for the exceptional "purchase of rare specimens not obtainable by donation."

Hornaday did not join in the resulting celebrations. Informed that his lack of administrative experience barred him from serving as the Zoo's first director, he had offered to work for a six-month trial period during which he would resign if he committed a single error of judgment. Langley, with firm ideas of his own on the Zoo's future, refused the wager, and Hornaday resigned in June 1890. In 1896 he became the New York Zoological Park's first director, and by the time he died at the age of 83 in 1937, he had earned for himself the unofficial title of dean of American zoo directors and, for his zoo, a reputation that the National Zoo long coveted.

Meanwhile, Frank Baker, curator of the National Museum's Department of Comparative Anatomy, was appointed the Zoo's first superintendent. He began "to lay out the park and endeavor to make some provision . . . for these animals under our windows [outside the Smithsonian Castle]. They are apt to be a trifle offensive in hot weather. . . ." That was among the least of his worries, however, as crowds closed in on the animals during the torpid Washington summer. A few years before, a bison, infuriated by teasing, poking visitors, had broken through its fence and nearly gored a nursemaid and her 3-year-old charge. The *Post* had clamored for more substantial enclosures to protect the animals from the public, as well as the public from the animals.

The Zoo's maintenance appropriation was severely cut the second year and its authority to purchase animals withdrawn, perhaps because only $17,000 of the previous year's allocation had been spent, or perhaps, as William M. Mann later explained, the newly elected members of the House "knew nothing of the park." The Smithsonian had to advance money from its own coffers to feed animals and buy supplies for workmen, receiving only partial reimbursement by a special congressional appropriation.

Langley's hopes of breeding threatened North American species disappeared with this cutback of congressional support. Sub-

sequently he ordered the entire park opened to the public in an effort to "excite the enthusiasm of the people." He directed the Zoo to give "prominence to native races, keeping the others quite subordinate," and insisted that the animals be kept in as natural a setting as possible. Frederick Law Olmsted, the designer of New York's Central Park, was hired to preserve the landscape and to disguise fencing as best he could. People soon began flocking to the Zoo.

Lacking adequate funds to increase its collection, the Zoo relied on gifts, barter, and privately financed expeditions. Langley enlisted the Army and other branches of government in his efforts to secure specimens, a precedent his successors willingly followed. U.S. Presidents and foreign heads of state donated exotic species, while native animals and former pets, such as monkeys, came in from Americans everywhere. Langley's close friend Alexander Graham Bell donated several mandarin ducks; "Buffalo Bill" Cody's offer of 18 bison was declined, however, due to lack of space on the Mall. Gifts from U.S. agencies abroad brought in such rarities as Cuban crocodiles and a Tasmanian wolf with three young in her pouch.

Once, during its early days, an animal dealer offered the Zoo a kangaroo for $75. The Zoo could not buy it, but a local animal dealer could and did, subsequently arranging to trade it to the Zoo for guinea pigs to feed his carnivorous birds. Charging 15 cents a guinea pig, it took the Zoo three years to retire the mortgage on the kangaroo.

William Blackburne, the head keeper, oversaw that trade. An expert animal handler, firm disciplinarian, and gifted storyteller, he provided much of the Zoo's starch for its first half-century. Accepting his position on January 29, 1891, for $83.33 a month, Blackburne reputedly quit the circus, married, and gave up drinking all on the same day. In 53 years, he did not take off a day for vacation or for illness. When an employee once asked for a holiday to get married, Blackburne is said to have replied that getting married required only 10 minutes.

Not until just before World War II did the Zoo hire Carter H. Anthony, its first full-time veterinarian. Up to that time, it had relied on government agencies for autopsies, and Blackburne had served as animal doctor as well as head keeper. A lion, rejected by a circus because of "incurable mange," had responded to Blackburne's sweet-oil-and-

Reflecting the need for urban recreation, zoos have traditionally served as popular settings for promotional activities and festive programs, such as the jazz concert and Isadora Duncan-inspired dance, above. The polar bears' reactions to this early '20s show are not on record.

sulphur treatments and spent many healthy years at the Zoo. Legend has it that some elephants acquired a taste for his gin-and-ginger chasers after mustard plasters for stomachaches. They appeared to feign digestive ailments until Blackburne prudently discontinued the chaser. At least one fastidious tiger had licked his dose of castor oil from his own coat, which Blackburne had deliberately soaked with the medicine.

For all Blackburne's craft and skill, however, the fledgling Zoo's survival was constantly challenged by politics, tight money and space, disease, climatic extremes, and ignorance of wild animals' needs. As many as one animal in 10 died every year, a representative mortality rate for zoos of the day. Rabies struck in 1895, distemper in 1897, foot-and-mouth disease in 1898. Blustery winters claimed parrots, flamingos, and other tropical creatures. Arctic natives succumbed to summer heat and malaria. Animals escaped from poorly constructed enclosures (one of them, a beaver, eluded his captors despite a trail of felled trees in his wake along Rock Creek). The bear yards and dens in the old granite quarry were "too damp in winter and too hot in summer for the health of the animals," wrote Baker. Animals that had

lived continents apart in the wild were housed, for lack of space, under one roof. "Timid animals suffer greatly when put in a house with large carnivorous beasts," observed Baker. "The sight of such animals terrifies them, and the cries of creatures whom they instinctively recognize as their natural enemies sometimes affect them so that they die of fright."

Male and female animals usually lived in separate cages. Offspring from mated animals gladdened Zoo officials' hearts, but a captive breeding program was considered unnecessary as it was thought that the wild would always offer more specimens.

William M. Mann, a 39-year-old entomologist with impeccable scientific credentials, became director in 1925. At that time the Zoo numbered 1,619 animals, representing 517 species. Dr. Mann inherited an institution that had yet to live up to its promise, but he was determined that it should do so. His philosophy of professionalism in zoo management may have paralleled his businesslike approach to the spectacular expeditions he organized: "I have always had a distaste for mixing adventures with animal collecting," he said. "In my experience, people who have adventures generally get killed."

35

Possessed of natural charm and an instinct for using the media to his benefit, Mann could be considered the Zoo's first director of public relations and fund-raising. One day, while conducting a VIP-tour, Mann overheard a mynah bird ask U.S. Budget Director General H. M. Lord, "How about the appropriation?" "That's impertinent," exclaimed Lord. The mynah rejoined, "So's your old man." Mann promised to investigate the bird's educational background, and the Zoo received an extra $30,000 appropriation.

Mann convinced automobile magnate Walter P. Chrysler to donate $50,000 for the Zoo's first animal-collecting expedition to East Africa. After six months, on October 24, 1926, the Chrysler ship docked at Boston, bearing 2,000 animals including a purple-faced monkey, elephant shrews, the largest leopard ever captured, rare African antelopes, and two young giraffes, one of which promptly kicked Blackburne. The head keeper denied that it hurt, however, claiming it "a pleasure to be kicked by a giraffe on its way to my own zoo!"

Although the Depression strained the Zoo's daily operations, laborers assigned by the Work Planning and Job Assignment Committee completed routine repairs. Then, in 1935, Mann received a telephone call from his friend Harold L. Ickes, Secretary of the Interior and head of the Public Works Administration. "He told me that we had been allotted $870,000, the biggest appropriation for new construction we'd ever had," Mann wrote in the *National Geographic*. "I nearly dropped the receiver."

The money built the Elephant House, the Small Mammal House, and a new wing for the Bird House. The Federal Project for the Arts provided rich embellishment to the Zoo's buildings and grounds, including floor mosaics in the Elephant and Lion Houses, painted murals of the Nile for the hippopotamuses, and sculptures of a giant anteater and tumbling red-granite bears.

Mann wasted no time filling the new buildings. In 1937, with a $35,000 grant from the National Geographic Society, he collected hog badgers and Komodo dragons in the East Indies. Malcolm Davis, head keeper of birds, traveled to Antarctica in 1939, collecting several species of penguin for the Zoo. In 1940, Harvey S. Firestone, Jr., the automobile tire manufacturer, contributed $15,000 to the Zoo's last great animal-collecting expedition, this one to Liberia. Before Mann returned

with pygmy hippos, monkeys, small duiker antelope, rare birds, and reptiles, Germany had invaded the Netherlands.

World War II's effect on the Zoo was as pervasive and severe as it was on the rest of society. Animal keepers went off to war, and venomous snakes were shipped to inland zoos, lest they escape through shattered glass in the event of an attack. Gas rationing discouraged visitors, and the threat of German submarines halted shipment of wild animals.

The postwar period saw behind-the-scenes improvements, including new quarters for the Zoo policemen. Their old one-room office over the Lion House had prompted the disquieting sign, "Lost Children Will Be Taken to the Lion House."

The number of Zoo visitors surged to 3.5 million in 1950—more than toured the White House, the Lincoln Memorial, or any Smithsonian museum. Moreover, surveys proved its character as a national zoo: more than half the visitors were tourists living outside the Washington area.

As Mann had greatly expanded the Zoo's acquisitions, so Theodore H. Reed, the Zoo veterinarian who became director in March 1958, set about intensifying one of the Zoo's original purposes—that of scientific research. In this venture he enjoyed the support of Smithsonian Secretary Leonard Carmichael, a psychologist best known for his contribution to the understanding of neonatal behavior.

Dr. Reed took over a zoo whose grounds were covered with poison ivy and whose buildings, including the hospital built in 1916, badly needed repairs. Indeed, the administration building was so infested with termites that not even a hungry anteater could save damaged photographic files.

As veterinarian, Reed had felt the pinch of the Zoo's budget. As director, he insisted on the only preventive medicine the Zoo could afford: the meticulous cleaning of animal quarters and attention to nutrition. Record-keeping practices slowly improved, and Reed ordered explanatory signs placed on every cage for the public's information. (Such an attempt under Mann's supervision had gone awry when an elephant wiped his name off the placard and swallowed the last drop of red paint from the can.)

Up to this time, little money had existed for public education, much less for research. Faced with the same financial constrictions as his predecessors, Reed used whatever means he could, including TV appearances,

Easter at the Zoo, circa 1905. Traditionally the busiest weekend of the year, thousands of visitors **such as those gathered on Lion Hill, above, still flock to the park on this spring holiday.**

to gain publicity and solicit funds. Finally, after Reed pleaded the Zoo's case before the Cleveland Park Citizens' Association in 1958, the Friends of the National Zoo (FONZ) formed to "promote the development of an educational service which would utilize all effective contemporary media." Today, FONZ coordinates all Zoo volunteer resources and contributes concession proceeds to support a variety of scientific activities, internships, and fellowship programs. The Zoo's recent FONZ-financed conference on animal pathology was a first in the United States.

In the early '60s the U.S. space program stirred interest in advanced medical research which depended on animals such as chimpanzees that resembled man biologically. At the same time the public was becoming increasingly sensitive to environmental needs, and concern for endangered species was mounting. Reed and others realized that zoos, which absorbed only a small percentage of all the animals taken from the wild, would have to become net producers rather than consumers of animals. Zoological research, so long

considered a luxury, was coming into its own.

In 1964, S. Dillon Ripley, an ornithologist, became Smithsonian Secretary, announcing soon after the Zoo's expansion into animal behavior and conservation research. Within a year the Zoo had raised enough money to hire John F. Eisenberg, an internationally renowned ethologist, to head the new Office of Zoological Research. Led by Reed and Dr. Eisenberg and with Ripley's enthusiastic support, a team of scientists concentrates on research that will advance the Zoo's knowledge of animal management through study of behavior in the wild.

While still offering recreation to area residents and visitors from all over the world, the National Zoo has won a place of distinction within the research community. Past, present, and future philosophies seem to converge symbolically in the Elephant House, whose pygmy hippos have sent progeny to nearly every zoo in the nation. Near one entrance hangs a brass memorial to "The Good Elephant Dunk," a reminder of the Zoo's difficult beginnings. □

LIVING SPACES

Epitomizing the new look and new thought at the National Zoo, this three-ring theater for lions and tigers allows viewers to peer directly into the fun and drama of the animals' lives. Lions claim the largest of the three spaces, right background; yellow and white tigers command the other two.

The grand old Lion House which originally stood at this site was the Zoo's first permanent structure, built in 1893. To visitors in those days it seemed a wondrous (if slightly overcrowded) ark for rhinos, hippos, alligators, and what-have-you, as well as lions. But in later, conscience-raised times, the public protested: "All those animals behind bars!" That impetus, translated into funds from Congress—plus the Zoo's recognition of its scientific and exhibition destiny—allowed implementation of the 1960s' master plan. Thus bloomed this new structure of concrete, turf, and strategic fencing.

Yet, the perennial question: "Can't they jump out?" Clearing the 4-foot wall with its two strands of electric wire would be possible for any cat. But it would then land in a 26-by-18-foot moat and be rounded up by a keeper. All of which has happened on at least one occasion.

At "Lion Hill" a prime objective has been the successful rearing of certain exotic feline species. With the white tigers, the hope is to create a perfect specimen without the physical deficiencies that have been caused by inbreeding. With the Atlas lions—on loan from Morocco—perpetuation of the line is the thrust, as only about 40 of them remain in the world. When the Zoo's first successful litters were produced in 1977, the Ambassador of Morocco made a formal, grateful visit to the Zoo: mission accomplished.

*　　*　　*

Although no sane cat would think it Africa or India, the Zoo's new William M. Mann Lion-Tiger Exhibit, above, offers naturalized spaces for playing, courting, or contemplating. At right, white tigers splash, wrestle with a beer keg. Atlas lions, left and below, are segregated by family lest females fight. Cats rotate out of dens selectively; viewers get eye-level view of social behavior. Below, a yellow tiger demonstrates its narrow-ledge capabilities at poolside.

It was like quickly putting together a palace for lovers from a distant planet; no one quite knew what would outrage or amuse the heavenly pair or how to keep them happy. They were, in fact, giant pandas, gifts from the people of China. The first problem in 1972 was how to house them.

The decision was reached to convert Delicate Hoofed Stock House Number One into an indoor-outdoor palazzo, fast. This structure was adaptable to the new purpose; it was air conditioned and centrally located. In it an 80-foot-long glass wall was built to separate adoring people from adorable pandas.

When the enclosure was ready and the crates opened, the newly arrived male panda seemed slightly disinclined to enter his new world. The female, however, was all too willing to perform. Within the first two years of occupancy, her acts of mayhem included roughing a keeper, reaching the top of the outside wall and nearly escaping. She hurled a 50-pound tub so strenuously against the glass that the *outer* panel was spiderwebbed.

Nonetheless, Ling-Ling has her charming side: she has not given up the old trick of putting her finished feeding pan atop her head. Hsing-Hsing has also lost some shyness: below, he delights in his pool.

An oriental sense of tranquility pervades the Gardens of the Pandas in the spring. The grass is lush, and the willows drip with new leaves. Indeed, some observers are surprised that over the years the pandas have lost their rambunctiousness and their passion for new toys. Yet, though these gardens are but an imitation of Imperial China, should anyone wonder that an imperial pair would choose to appear sedate?

*   *   *

Raised viewing area, above, affords view into pandas' fenced paddocks, opposite, connected via chain-linked "moon gate," below. The 8-foot-high wall with gate encourages communication.

The Zoo's master plan provided five times more neck-stretching room for its giraffes than in their old pens. Rhinos, hippos, elephants, and bears also got more elbow room—though some seemed loath to ramble across the unfamiliar spaces to take advantage of the freer yards and cooling pools.

The African black rhinoceros' yard, pictured at right, incorporates a slightly suspicious-looking cliff that once offered perches to the deft feet of auodad sheep. It represents not the new, scientific era but the intuitive old—yet why reject it if it still offers a good place to scratch? These gunnite rocks were the idea of a German zoo owner named Hagenbeck who, at the turn of the century, devised fantastic landscapes of fake mountains, moats, and water courses. Zoos all over the world found his fantasies sensible, his techniques practical and inexpensive, and began installing such systems.

Beyond amenity, security is necessary for the enclosures of these huge beasts. In 1974, before the new structures were completed, a 5-foot-high fence surrounded the elephants' yard. Nancy, feeling perhaps that mate Zimbo did not return her elephantine affections, shoved him over the fence into the moat outside. Today's yard, many times larger, boasts a contoured wall that could contain a herd of trailer trucks.

A peculiarly Washington problem for all animals, and particularly for the polar bears, is the oppressive heat of summer. Their new, specially designed, ice-simulating environment closer to Rock Creek may help, but the dens' cool recesses and the pools' depths clearly provide more real relief: the bears spend most of the warm months indoors or submerged. Not wishing viewers to be defeated by this behavior, Director Reed ordered architects to add windows for subsurface observation.

Though apparently quite comfortable in their spacious, modernized quarters (as opposed to the restrictive cages they formerly occupied), the five resident polar bears have yet to bring forth cubs from the privacy of the dens. Cries of infants have been heard on the monitoring system, however, so zoo keepers know that in the new spaces old, life-giving processes are at work.

*   *   *

Like many Washingtonians, the polar bears have the summertime problem of a quirky filtration system in their pool.

Looking ready to charge, the rhino at left top is, in fact, more likely to walk round and round in circles, left center, because of the cramped space it grew accustomed to before the new yard was built. At back of elephants' yard, left bottom, can be seen their pool and that of the hippo, top.

"Holy Smoke, the kookaburra Hilton!" exclaimed a visiting zoologist when he first saw the National Zoo's great flight cage, built in 1964. Though it now houses none of Australia's loud-mouthed kookaburras, its wire netting still gives a great variety of exotic birds the impression of unlimited freedom for flying and breeding (below).

Birds admitted are limited to those that can tolerate Washington's winters, a list that includes Inca terns, Guanay cormorants, pheasants, and magpies. In icy months, flight cage birds find food stored in heated, artificial logs. Another criterion for birds' admission is compatibility; fierce fighters like hawks stay in other outdoor cages.

Bald eagles have inherited an airy Victorian creation where they dwell in solitary splendor. For them this isolation from other possibly competitive species works well: in 1973 they made history by producing the third captive bald eagle born in recent years; and then produced another eaglet in 1978.

Sparrows liked the look of the flight cage and wanted in. Getting the hang of the "impenetrable" wires, they found they could slip through. Now they're members. Predators, however, are successfully excluded . . . except for humans. One of these, apparently believing that a cage exists only to be broken out of, cut a big hole in the net with clippers. None of the birds followed him out.

*   *   *

Six parabolic arches, top left, and a 90-foot center shaft, opposite, support the flight cage's fine wire netting. As if with spread wings, it hovers over a crannied rock face behind the main Bird House, built in 1932. The flight room of the Bird House, top right, offers a lush, skylit setting for indoor birds. Bald eagles and other raptors used to share the old pavilion-like cage, above right, but only after the latter group's banishment did successful eagle breeding occur, above.

Consistent with the strange law of zoos that people are traditionally most attracted to animals that wriggle, the Reptile House is the National Zoo's most visited building. It is also the Zoo's most compelling and intriguing structure, its red tile roof rising above façades decorated with images of the fascinating beasts that dwell therein. Designed in the 1930s when craftsmen were lavishing their talents on federal architecture, the building's detailing also benefited from the work of local sculptors.

Visitors come to see the special worlds of such select reptiles and amphibians as Cuban crocodiles, monitors, gila monsters, various geckos, caimans, turtles, frogs, and snakes and snakes and snakes (pythons, rattlers, boas, cobras, copperheads, and water moccasins, among others).

Most of the animals in the building's six lines of indoor exhibits live in simulated tropical settings—with Spanish moss hanging from real or man-made trees. Whereas some snakes and lizards require darkness during daytime hours, others have body clocks that call for the opposite.

One of the projects which Reptile Curator Dale Marcellini is overseeing involves the reticulated Burmese python. To see if the female python followed set incubation patterns, a researcher monitored the temperatures both of the coil which the snake forms around her eggs, and of the cage. The mother uses muscular contractions to raise her body temperature and thus heat her cluster of eggs. These twitchings occur much like shivering in humans: the lower the cage's temperature, the more rapid the rate of contractions.

Other Reptile House inhabitants are also sensitive to surroundings. When keeper leader Mike Davenport replaced plastic vegetation with real stuff in a red spotted newt's cage, the previously unproductive amphibian deposited eggs onto a neatly folded leaf.

*　　*　　*

To enter the Reptile House, top, one pulls open a pair of massive oak doors, above, decorated with sculpted panels of lizards and dinosaurs. One of the panels depicts a stegosaurus, left, which like many reptiles of today was brutal-looking but basically inoffensive. So come on in without fear.

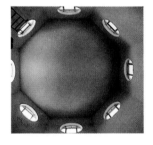

Beneath the Reptile House's red-tiled roof, left, and its lantern-like tower, above, curators have established exhibits of different reptile environments, like the crocodile swamp scene at top left. Reptiles in stone and concrete, shown in other illustrations on this page, occupy niches in surprising places around the building's exterior.

When Elton Howe retired, he wondered what to do with the clock that had stood so tall in front of his jewelry shop in downtown Washington. Each of the clock's four faces was decorated with a lion's head with ring in teeth—so why not, he thought, give the clock to the National Zoo? That he did; it now stands near the gift shop, opposite page.

Both that clock and the remarkable animal glockenspiel shown opposite—willed by a local doctor—illustrate that citizens share the yearning for a special ambiance at the Zoo. Some gifts need to be dragged forth, however. Smithsonian Secretary Ripley was glad enough to let Montreal's Expo borrow the enormous stone eagle from New York's demolished Pennsylvania Station that had been granted to the Smithsonian. But when Expo closed and the eagle's possessors were disinclined to see it fly away, strong diplomatic action was called for.

Today the eagle's head and back, right, polished by climbing children, gleam in the sun. Like the adults who take a more sophisticated view of the carefully created harmony between animals and structures and amenities at the National Zoo, the children find zoo-going a feast for all senses. □

In the 1930s, Public Works Administration sculptors produced beguiling figures such as the anteater, below right, to enhance the Zoo's grounds. The precedent for such art had been set by turn-of-the-century sculptures atop the Monkey House, including the terra cotta bear. That tradition continues with the 1976 "Happy Frog," opposite, and a ceramic mural, below.

The glockenspiel above plays either by carillon-neurs' fists or automatic tape; either way, the four 4-foot-high animals move (elephant raises trunk, flaps ears) and bells ring out tunes like "Hail to the Redskins." For years Howe came to the Zoo to clean and repair his clock, below.

STOCKING THE ZOO

THE ART OF ACQUISITION

Thomas Crosby

Before today's era of animal conservation, American zoos replenished their stock primarily through animal-collecting expeditions to far-flung corners of the world and through dealers and other animal collectors. Accompanied by native bearers, such collectors trekked through steamy jungles or across arid plains, combating disease, insects, and occasional attacks by wild animals. Highly romanticized by local newspapers, radio programs, Frank Buck's movies and his book *Bring 'em Back Alive,* these pre-World War II excursions were the most efficient way for a zoo to acquire, in one fell swoop, hundreds of different mammals, reptiles, and birds.

New animals had to be obtained to balance out the frequent deaths. In those days, an average of one-fourth the number of animals residing at the National Zoo died each year. Expeditions and purchases, of course, did not account for all the incoming animals. Foreign dignitaries and wealthy benefactors often donated animals, as did U.S. Presidents who received them as state gifts. Ordinary citizens donated pets as well. Some species reproduced in captivity; others were obtained through trades with other zoos. But whatever the source, the wild provided most of the Zoo newcomers. "There they must be pursued and captured," declared William M. Mann

Zoo Director Reed arrives in India in 1960 on mission to acquire a white tiger.

who, as director of the National Zoo from 1925 to 1956, led expeditions to Africa, Cuba, British Guiana, the East Indies, and Argentina. Dr. Mann brought back more than 3,100 animals, some of which became the founding parents of generations of zoo-born animals.

Such expeditions were challenging, dangerous undertakings. The drama involved first locating the animal, then capturing it without injury, caring for it as well as possible, transporting it in a cage through rugged terrain to the nearest seaport, and, finally, launching it on a lengthy voyage over thousands of miles of ocean. Many animals died, either during capture or in passage, for temporary cages on deck exposed the captives to all kinds of inclement weather. Nor did methods improve very rapidly.

In the twenties it was catch as catch can. On his first expedition in 1926, Mann received a permit authorizing his party to capture specimens of nearly all the game in the territory then called Tanganyika. The permit also allowed, when necessary, the killing of the mother in order to capture the young, a policy deplored by today's conservationists but one that animal dealers and collectors had followed for centuries.

Local people did most of the actual capturing of animals on these expeditions. But delivering wild animals to the person heading the safari was easier said than done. In India, for example, members of the Forest Department of Assam once hacked an 8-mile road through dense forest to transport a rare one-horned rhinoceros to the nearest railroad line. On another expedition, a female pygmy hippopotamus caught in Liberia underwent an even more grueling odyssey. A 300-pound cage was built to carry the 400-pound hippo, then the entire load lugged on a two-and-a-half-day, 40-mile journey to the nearest town. From there the hippo was driven 50 miles down the African coast by truck, loaded onto a boat, rowed two miles out to sea, lifted on board ship by a derrick, led down into the hold, and then fed nothing but potatoes for three weeks after all the greens had spoiled. The hippo, named Matilda, disembarked at Norfolk, Virginia, and journeyed to Washington via Railway Express. Matilda not only survived her ordeal but has borne nine offspring since her arrival in 1940 and has lived longer at the National Zoo than any other mammal.

Mann's 1926 expedition, the most successful in the Zoo's history, captured 1,353

A worker in Peking, top, helps unload one of the musk oxen shipped from America. Ling-Ling, above, reclines in her shipping cage.

animals including impala, a greater kudu, an eland, three white-bearded gnus, and the first pair of giraffes ever exhibited in Washington. Mann's health after World War II prevented him from leading any further expeditions.

Theodore H. Reed, who became director of the Zoo in 1958, recalls that he visualized himself "going into the deep, dark, mysterious jungle after animals, wrestling pythons to the ground, and living with the natives in safari camps. But times change, and while I wanted to be like Frank Buck, you just couldn't do it anymore. Today, you go to a country for a specific animal. You can't just pick up any animals you happen to see along the way and bring them back."

While Mann had battled insects, heat, disease, and other dangers, Dr. Reed, on his first mission, encountered bureaucracy, the modern hazard of animal collecting. He traveled in 1960 to Rewa, India, to pick up Mohini, a 2-year-old white tigress being purchased by a businessman for $10,000 as a gift to the children of the United States. Although Reed carried a letter from the Indian Ministry of Commerce and Industry stating that the tiger could be exported, the Ministry of Food and Agriculture in New Delhi refused to honor it. Calling Mohini a national treasure even though she was born at the Palace and not caught in the wild, the ministry ordered

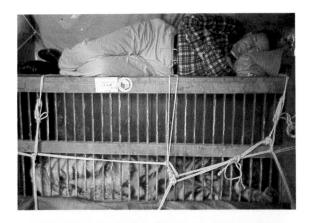

A weary Dr. Reed sleeps atop Mohini's cage enroute to the United States. Bottom, the tiger is formally presented to President Eisenhower on the White House grounds.

customs officials to prohibit the animal's departure. Accompanied by officials from the U.S. Embassy, Reed spent several tense hours at the ministry proving that his permit was valid and convincing the officials that Mohini's departure would not endanger India's supply of white tigers.

It took 11 men to carry Mohini and her cage to the waiting plane. An exhausted Reed and his assistant took turns guarding the tiger day and night. Finally, on December 5, 1960, Mohini was formally presented to President Eisenhower as a gift to the children of the United States in ceremonies on the White House lawn.

Reed's experience in India presaged the change that swept the world in the 1960s and 1970s, spelling the end of wholesale importation of animals into the United States and the cessation of costly animal-gathering expeditions. National and international wildlife-preservation organizations proliferated, along with numerous laws governing the

hunting, capture, exportation, and importation of animals in countries where such legislation had never before existed. Today, the U.S. Endangered Species Act of 1973 and the Convention on International Trade in Endangered Species of Wild Fauna and Flora govern the export, import, and even the habitats of more than 600 imperiled species.

On the federal level, four powerful government agencies play a role in animal commerce: Health, Education and Welfare concerns itself with diseases that humans could contract from animals; Agriculture worries about the welfare of the animals and the spread of diseases between domestic and wild specimens; Commerce holds jurisdiction over marine mammals; and Interior seeks to protect the animals and their environments from exploitation. In addition, several states, including New York, California, and Florida, have passed their own laws regulating animal commerce and transportation.

Indeed, today's legal requirements entwine the acquisition of animals with considerable red tape. Zoos chafe at the paperwork, yet they support the main thrust of the regulations. Even so, the American Association of Zoological Parks and Aquariums favors easing some of the requirements because, it points out, the shipping of animals to and from qualified zoos, which is heavily regulated, is for the purpose of increasing, not decreasing, the species' population.

A basic law of economics also affects the acquisition of exotic animals. As in any marketplace, supply and demand govern the animal trade. Prolific captive breeders, such as African lions, glut the market and are relatively inexpensive. Other animals, such as the African elephant, may cost more than $12,000 because they are both difficult to obtain in the wild and seldom breed in captivity. Animal prices generally have skyrocketed also because of import and export restrictions. Since 1973 the price of a lesser panda has doubled to $3,500. A Chilean flamingo that formerly cost $125 now sells for $750, and a lineated barbet, a nonmigratory tropical bird that could be purchased for $20 in 1972, cost $300 in 1978. The American Association of Zoological Parks and Aquariums regularly publishes a list of surplus animals available from different zoos, with asking prices, and animal dealers circulate their own lists which resemble newspaper supermarket ads.

Prior to the 1973 Act, American Presidents

contributed substantially to stocking the National Zoo. President Grover Cleveland set a precedent in 1887 when he gave a golden eagle to the Smithsonian's Department of Living Animals, the predecessor of the National Zoological Park. Since then, 15 Presidents have donated a total of 98 animals, including opossums, raccoons, turkeys (one dyed red, white, and blue), coyotes, and rabbits. In accepting such ordinary species, the Zoo's graciousness and patience were rewarded by the presentation as well of rare and exotic animals. Harry Truman donated an albino kangaroo and birds of paradise. Theodore Roosevelt gave the Zoo a Somali ostrich, and Dwight Eisenhower presented it with bear cubs from Korea.

Foreign governments and dignitaries often donate animals as a gesture of friendship and political alliance, as was most notably demonstrated in 1972 with the gift of two giant pandas from the people of the People's Republic of China. Other state gifts have included Arabian oryxes from Saudi Arabia, goldfish from the Japanese Imperial Collection, two Indian rhinoceroses from Assam, a pair of okapi from the Belgian Congo (shortly before Belgium abandoned colonial rule in Africa), kiwis and tuataras from New Zealand, and Komodo dragons from Indonesia.

The 1973 Endangered Species Act precipitated a three-year lull in state gifts. Sri Lanka ended this hiatus by presenting Shanthi, an Asiatic elephant, to the children of America in 1976. Asiatic elephants joined the endangered species list shortly before Shanthi's departure, and paperwork documenting the fact that she had been found abandoned in the wild had to be hastily prepared. Discovered away from the herd, without her mother, Shanthi had lived in a Sri Lankan elephant orphanage before being shipped to her new home.

As the country's representative zoo, the National Zoo enjoys other types of unique gifts as well. Smokey bear, for example, a cinnamon-colored black bear rescued from a forest fire in New Mexico's Lincoln National Forest, came to the Zoo in 1950. The cub, a living symbol of forest fire prevention, received such lavish fan mail that the Forest Service presented him with a secretarial staff, and the Post Office with his own zip code.

Another famous zoo personality, Ham the chimpanzee, rode 155 miles into the stratosphere aboard a Redstone rocket on January 31, 1961, pushing levers when lights flashed and thus guiding his craft to a safe landing in the Atlantic. The National Aeronautics and Space Administration proclaimed that Ham's flight "verified the feasibility of manned space flight through operational tests of the Mercury life-support system." In 1963 the Air Force gave the chimponaut to the Zoo, retiring him with full military honors.

While "official" animals may readily find a home along the Rock Creek banks, citizens will no longer find the Zoo receptive to the gift of a pet snake or raccoon. Although Director Mann espoused an "NRA"—never refuse anything—policy, limited cage space and the spiraling costs of animal feed have forced the Zoo to become more selective.

This policy of selectiveness affects animals offered for sale or trade as well. Like many zoos today, the National Zoo is establishing breeding programs, and unless an animal fits into a specific program, the Zoo may reject it.

"Now," explains Reed, "if we are offered an animal, we discuss it among ourselves. We decide where we will put it, how we will care for it, whether it will be a good exhibit animal, and how it will fit into the breeding program. Today there is far less spontaneous acquisition than before."

Captive breeding programs command top priority at most modern zoos, and have succeeded in saving several animal species from extinction. Père David's deer, wisent (European buffalo), Przewalski's wild horse, and a subspecies, the Atlas lion, no longer exist in their native habitat. They can be seen only in zoos and private animal preserves.

Limited paddock space at the Zoo inter-

A white tiger cub born at the Zoo displays crossed eyes, one of the genetic oddities that may result from breeding for white tigers.

feres with the breeding of many species of hoofed stock by restricting the size of the herd. Fortunately the 3,150-acre Conservation and Research Center at Front Royal, Virginia, offers fields spacious enough to pasture large numbers of Bactrian camels, Grant's zebras, scimitar-horned oryxes, Eld's and Père David's deer, and Persian onagers.

"We have to look at captive animals as a trust for future generations," says Reed. "Obviously, we're in a race against time. As more and more animals in the world are threatened, the use of zoos as survival centers will take on increasing importance."

Births in zoos among rare and endangered species must keep pace with or exceed the number of deaths. The number of births at the Zoo has slightly exceeded the number of deaths for several years (994 births or hatchings in 1978 as compared to 549 deaths). Much of this life-and-death activity occurs within the bird collection, partly because birds on the average live a shorter time than mammals, and partly because the Zoo exhibits more birds than any other animal. In 1978 the National Zoo had 915 birds, 997 mammals, 481 reptiles, and 88 amphibians. Roughly three-fourths of the new animals in 1978 came from the 994 births; only one-fourth were acquired by purchase, gift, trade,

or loan. While births outnumber deaths, the Zoo is still striving to improve its captive breeding programs.

Cooperative loan agreements between zoos offer one hope. In 1930, the last Atlas lion seen in the wild was killed in Morocco. The royal family owned the only surviving lions, and eventually gave these unusual cats to the Rabat zoo. From their group of 30, the Rabat zoo sent four Atlas lions to the National Zoo to form a breeding pool, thereby reducing the chance that a single calamity could wipe out all of the tawny beasts. The three females and sole male quickly produced six offspring, including four males, one year after arriving in the United States. The Rabat zoo owns all the youngsters and, along with the National Zoo, may set up other breeding pools.

Most of the large American zoos operate similar breeding loan programs. In 1978 at least 56 different institutions were housing 154 of the National Zoo's animals, including Burmese pythons, Hawaiian nene geese, burrowing owls, scimitar-horned oryxes, dorcas gazelles, golden marmosets, orangutans, and brush turkeys.

The Hawaiian nene geese, once near extinction, have bred so well in captivity that they have been reintroduced to the wild. In 1978 the National Zoo technically owned 28

Malcolm Davis, left, then the Zoo's head bird keeper, and a helper prepare food for animals captured on a 1937 National Geographic Society-sponsored animal-collecting expedition.

Indian Ambassador Vijaya Pandit poses in 1950 with pachyderms Shanti and Ashok, gifts from her country to the American people.

of these birds, scattered among nine zoos.

Currently, approximately 450 specimens are involved in breeding loans to and from the National Zoo. These include Rothschild's mynahs from Los Angeles; Caribbean flamingos from Buffalo; white-winged wood ducks from England; Bactrian camels from Cleveland, Minnesota, San Antonio, and Michigan; and Persian onagers from San Diego, Baltimore, Dallas, and Los Angeles.

Some breeding loans involve one-for-one exchanges for the purpose of establishing new blood lines and preventing inbreeding. Other swaps, such as those in November 1978 involving the golden marmosets, become more complicated. This particular trade ultimately included dealings between the National Zoo and zoos in Fort Worth, Los Angeles, Seattle, and Lincoln, Nebraska.

The marmoset program began at the Zoo in 1969 with only two breeding pairs, yet by 1978 the Zoo had recorded more than 100 marmoset births. This success takes on even more significance considering that in 1975 only 250 of the small, golden creatures existed in their native habitat, Brazil.

Breeding exotic animals in captivity always involves more than simply putting together a male and female of the same species and letting nature take its course. Dozens of often obscure factors can affect an animal's ability or willingness to reproduce: age, hormone levels, cage space, compatibility, estrous cycle, climate, diet, health, family relationships, and the conditions under which the animal was raised.

Should a pair of animals not be compatible, zoos search for more attractive mates. Butch,

a male orangutan, and Jennie, a female, spent 11 years at the National Zoo without showing any sexual interest in each other once Butch reached sexual maturity (about 8). In the hope that other female orangutans might prove more stimulating to Butch, he was sent to the Franklin Park zoo in Boston. After failing to exhibit any sexual activity there, Butch was eventually moved to the Cheyenne Mountain Zoological Park in Colorado Springs, where he fathered over half a dozen orangutans.

To replace Butch, the National Zoo traded Leonard, a male gorilla, for Archie, an adult male orangutan with a proven breeding record. Within 10 months after Archie's arrival, Jennie was pregnant. Over the years the pair produced seven offspring.

Another breeding achievement—that between Tarun, a wild-caught Indian rhinoceros, and Raji, a captive-born female—illustrates the difficulties of captive breeding. In July 1968, when Tarun was 10 and Raji 5, they were put together for the first time. Although they spent seven hours of each day together during most of that summer, they exhibited no sexual interest in one another—perhaps because Raji was so young. Finally, in August 1970, Raji went into estrus. Both animals showed signs of sexual excitement, Raji whistling and Tarun dancing, snorting, and tossing his head in the air. Tarun mounted her several times, although never long enough to achieve conception.

For the next two years the rhinos were periodically put together with the same results: a lot of exertion but no success. In July 1972 the two animals were kept together overnight as FONZ volunteers, in three-hour

Ham the chimpanzee achieved suborbital flight aboard the Redstone rocket on January 31, 1961.

A flock of flamingos graces the waters off Inagua in the Bahamas. Captive breeding programs in the Caribbean—including Santo Domingo's—provide many zoos with these birds.

shifts, carefully recorded all activity. In September, the pair was observed breeding.

Later in the fall Raji failed to come into estrus and on January 30, 1974, delivered a 125-pound male. Named Patrick, it was the first surviving Indian rhinoceros ever born in a North American zoo.

Although zoos generally strive to maintain gene pools with different blood lines, in at least one celebrated case—that involving the white tiger Mohini—the Zoo purposely sought inbreeding. It was expected that Mohini's genes would produce white cubs if she were bred to another tiger possessing white genes. Mohini was first mated to Samson, her uncle and half-brother, a yellow tiger with white genes. One of their offspring, Ramana, a yellow male, later mated with his mother, producing two litters but only one survivor, Rewati, a white tigress. Very early in her life Rewati developed crossed blue eyes, which some scientists attribute to "inbreeding depression" caused by too little diversity in her blood lines. Her shorter legs and curved back may also have resulted from inbreeding, as white tigers grow faster and heavier than their yellow counterparts.

Because of the questions raised about inbreeding depression, zoos with white tigers are searching for yellow tigers to outbreed the species for genetic diversity. Offspring from such matings could be bred with high expectations that a white cub would result.

In contrast to promoting an increase in the breeding success of many of their species, zoos also sometimes face the responsibility of preventing the birth of surplus animals—especially members of the cat family. One of the pioneers in birth control for exotic animals was Clinton W. Gray, the National Zoo's senior veterinarian who retired in 1978. In 1974 Dr. Gray, along with Dr. U. S. Seal, a biochemist at the University of Minnesota, placed slow-leaking Depo-Provera pills in the shoulders of five female lions in a Virginia safari park. The scientists wished to stop the possibility of conception but not permanently damage the animals' ability to reproduce.

"We decided to try a chemical because it is reversible," said Gray. "You can't reverse castration, vasectomy, or hysterectomy. The pills prevent pregnancy for up to two and a half years." A pill costs only $150 a year compared to the estimated cost of $1,400 a year to feed an adult lion. Obviously, a zoo with too many lions must pay a very expensive food bill.

It appears important that the female lions continue to mate, even if pregnancy is prevented by chemical implant. In the past, when long separations were used to prevent conception, some females would not mate when reunited with males, let alone become pregnant. Another argument for this contraceptive program lies in the fact that castration of male lions can cause them to lose their manes.

Balanced against the prolific breeders are

the frustrating failures. Into this category falls the Zoo's most celebrated nonmating couple, Hsing-Hsing and Ling-Ling, the giant pandas. Volunteers and students have collected reams of panda behavioral data, noting the frequency and time spent by both pandas in such activities as scent marking, ball playing, or pacing about the concrete-and-glass interior of their $500,000 home or the spacious green yards outside.

When the pandas are put together in the same enclosure in the spring, tape recordings register their bleating and chirping sounds, and videotape cameras create a visual diary of their meetings. Ling-Ling was about 2½ years old in 1973, when the pair were first put together. She seemed eager to mate, but Hsing-Hsing, her junior by a half year, remained reluctant.

Zoologists did not view Hsing-Hsing's inexperience as abnormal, however. While nature may bestow on an animal the innate capacity for reproducing and ensuring the survival of the species, it often leaves to chance the matter of sexual orientation. In the wild, younger social animals may gain sexual prowess through watching older members of their species mate.

When Devra Kleiman, the Zoo's reproduction zoologist, visited China in 1978 to study panda mating behaviors, she learned that many pandas don't begin breeding until they are 6 or 7 years old. Some of China's pandas, in fact, did not produce litters until they were 10 years of age. And one female in her mid-20s had shown signs of estrus and could have possibly borne young. "If pandas can breed at age 20," says Dr. Kleiman, "it means the time we have left to breed them naturally has increased dramatically."

Artificial insemination of exotic animals is a growing science. Director Reed considers it "a very useful tool that we're going to have to develop." While zoos would prefer that their animals breed naturally, the difficulty, danger, and red tape of transporting live animals make artificial insemination an attractive alternative. The Peking zoo announced in the fall of 1978 that Cheung-Cheung, one of four female pandas artificially inseminated the previous spring, had given birth to two cubs after a 130-day gestation, although only one survived.

Eventually the National Zoo would like to computerize pertinent data on all of its animals, documenting family trees, medical histories, and individual idiosyncrasies. In-

For protection during shipping, flamingos' legs are wrapped and folded against their undersides. Birds are then placed in crates.

ternational Species Inventory System in Minnesota currently stores computerized data on zoo populations, enabling zoos to locate potential breeding partners for their specimens.

Zoos have come a long way since the days when directors, like old-fashioned horse traders, made deals in smoke-filled back rooms at annual conventions. Professionalism and cooperation now form the rule as zoos strive toward their crucial goal of successfully breeding and preserving the animals of the world. □

CAPTURING BONGOS

In 1969, the Zoo received a National Geographic Society grant to study and capture the bongo in Kenya's Abadare National Forest. This animal, one of the rarest of the forest antelopes, had seldom been captured before. Its large ears, moving constantly like antennae, warn it of approaching predators. Primarily nocturnal, bongos travel in small bands of up to 15 and are extremely wary.

Eight pit traps were dug along identified bongo trails over a period of two years. Since these animals are so sensitive to human disturbance, it took months before they resumed using the trails. But, at length, two males and a female fell into the traps. In each case, the animal was transferred to a small holding corral erected immediately after capture next to the pit trap. Here the animals remained for several weeks to accustom them to captivity.

Surprisingly enough, considering their shyness, the bongos quickly adapted to the presence of human beings and a changed life-style, becoming quite tame and gentle. After several months of further acclimatization on a farm near Nairobi, they were shipped to the United States along with an additional female acquired from a palm nut grower in West Africa.

They have bred and done reasonably well in their new home in Washington. □

Reed's Land Rover negotiating ruts after a heavy rain. Above, a concealed trap; below, a bongo in the acclimatization pen at trap site.

Workers at left maneuver a crate down a foggy trail to base camp. Above, a male munches on a carrot while still in Kenya. Marks at base of horns indicate time of capture and changes from its native diet and altitude. The bongo from West Africa, below, is coaxed into its shipping crate.

SECTION II
SHEPHERDS

KEEPER AND CURATOR

FRONT LINES OF ZOO WORK

Thomas Crosby

From the time he was 6 years old, growing up near the jungles of Panama, the world of Louis Walsh has revolved around snakes and other reptiles. His father gave him a baby crocodile, the start of a collection which eventually blossomed into some 50-odd specimens. Today he is a reptile keeper at the National Zoological Park and keeps a dozen snakes in the basement of his home.

Miles Roberts grew up in Canberra, Australia, where one could get out to the bush country in 10 minutes or so and see kangaroos, lizards, and exotic birds in the wild. After raising many snakes and birds as a child and coming to the United States as a university student, he took a volunteer summer job at the Zoo "just to be working with animals." Today he is curator of small mammals, currently helping design the new Ape House and overseeing construction details.

Keepers and curators at the National Zoo work closely together to ensure the physical and psychological health of the animals in their charge. Many have kept animals at home since their grade-school days and are, in a sense, fulfilling childhood dreams.

The 65 keepers provide much of the physical labor needed to maintain wild animals in captivity. They spend the greater part of their time on such duties as scrubbing cages, raking yards, feeding the animals, and keeping daily records of animal behavior. But more than that, experienced keepers can detect slight deviations in an animal's behavior that may be a subtle clue that an animal is ill or injured. The keeper, then, is the first line of defense in keeping the animal healthy.

Curators, on the other hand, consider long-range questions of policy relating to the animals. These can range from decisions on acquisition and breeding to those concerning educational materials, including the wording on signs. It could be said that the keepers manage individual specimens while the curators manage species. Such a definition, however, belies the many overlapping duties and concerns between the two positions.

*   *   *

A typical day in the life of an elephant keeper begins early in the morning with rather sophisticated interaction. Elephant House keeper Chris Mercer slips between the 4-inch-thick steel cage bars and walks up to

A hand-reared Inca tern perches on a willing head, above; at right, keeper Linda Mahn holds a red panda, distant cousin of the giant panda.

62

"Trooper" Walsh performs the daily chore of cleaning cages in the Reptile House. This task gives keepers a sense of the animals' well-being and is the first line of defense in health.

Nancy, a 25-year-old, 9-foot-tall female African elephant weighing more than three and a half tons. Nancy gyrates her sniffing trunk around the ankles of the 155-pound Mercer, careful not to touch him until he touches her, keeper-elephant etiquette Mercer has trained the elephants to observe. Only after Mercer strokes Nancy's leathery skin does the elephant place her sensitive trunk in Mercer's hand and accept his hand in her mouth, gestures similar to the way in which elephants greet each other in the wild.

Mercer repeats his stylized greeting with the two Asiatic elephants, Shanthi, 3, and Ambika, 28, who share another cage. After removing their chains, he orders them to "Line up." They shuffle to one side of the cage and stand docilely side by side while Mercer cleans up, shoveling dozens of pounds of elephant manure into a hand cart.

Being herd animals, elephants need social contact, which Mercer provides by his presence, as do other keepers and the two other elephants. In the wild, elephants frequently find themselves being pushed around, subordinated, by the more dominant elephants in a pattern that reinforces the herd's social structure. In much the same way, Mercer maintains dominance over the Zoo's elephants by enforcing commands such as "Lie down," "Back up," and an occasional thump with an elephant hook, a 2-foot-long wooden pole with a dull, curved metal hook and blunted metal spike on the end. The command "Back

up" is used when an elephant tries to test the dominance relationship by subtly crowding a keeper into a corner. "Lift leg" allows keepers to cut away the spongy, dead flesh on the sole of the elephant's foot or to trim its toenails, a pedicure that elephants in the wild perform by rubbing their feet against rocks.

Because of their size and strength, elephants and many other animals can be dangerous to work with. Good keepers must be consistent in their own behavior toward the animal in order to elicit predictable responses. They must establish a set work pattern, in essence becoming an integral part of the animals' landscape. While all the Zoo's animals react to consistency, the great apes, like the elephants, establish individual relationships with their keepers. Melanie Bond and Walter Tucker, keepers in the great ape section of the Small Mammal House, adhere to an established routine in greeting the Zoo's three lowland gorillas, three orangutans, and Ham, the single chimpanzee—the species of great ape considered the most intelligent and teachable. Both keepers enjoy great rapport with their charges.

The gorillas, Nikumba, Tomoka, and Femelle, greet Bond with a guttural grumble indicating a positive reaction and acceptance of her presence. Ham bares his teeth and jumps around the cage in excitement. Atjeh, the male orangutan born at the Zoo in 1966, lies down next to his cage bars and extends his arm through the bars as far as it will go so that Bond or Tucker can play with his fingers. Pensi, a female orangutan, thrusts her chin out for a chuck under her huge fold of flaccid flesh; Jennie, another female, maneuvers for a pat on the head or a tug at her lower lip.

Each of the apes insists on being greeted in the morning. If they feel ignored it triggers temper tantrums and unruly dispositions. While Chris Mercer maintains a position of dominance over the elephants, Bond and Tucker cultivate the trust and acceptance of the great apes, who have been known to reject a new keeper on sight. Some keepers in other zoos, however, have been able to dominate gorillas by imitating the mannerisms of a dominant gorilla in the wild.

"I'm not dominant to them," says Bond. "There are areas in which they look to me for leadership. When I pick up the hose, they watch and take their cues from me. When I start to hose down the right side of the cage, they stay on the left. When I say 'Move,' they go over to the right. I control when they get food, but they decide what and how much to eat. I decide whether they go outside or stay in, but they are in charge of what they do inside the cage. Sometimes they do what I want even though they aren't very happy about it. Then they show their displeasure by making noises, throwing whatever they can get hold of, or getting a mouthful of water and playing 'Let's wet the keeper.'"

Bond talks to the apes constantly, and it appears that they seek verbal praise from her when they respond correctly to her commands, an example of "positive conditioning." In addition to such verbal support, Bond will permit drinks from the water hose or hand out candy Life Savers. Conversely, Bond's "negative conditioning" includes withholding little favors or verbally chastising an ape for misbehavior.

The value of having verbal mastery over the great apes was dramatically demonstrated when Atjeh one day applied his active imagination to some browse—long branches given the apes to chew and pick bark from. Selecting the longest one (about 3 feet long), Atjeh climbed to the metal cage bars overhead and, with the branch, smashed an overhead light bulb. Picking up the broken glass and putting it in his mouth, Atjeh began prancing around his cage. When Bond discovered what had occurred, she summoned Atjeh to the cage bars with a stern voice and held out her hand. Atjeh opened his mouth

and the glass fell into Bond's open palm, fortunately before the orangutan had suffered any serious cuts.

Bond's awareness of the great apes' personalities and intelligence motivates her to invent games to provide physical and mental exercise and relieve their boredom. Jennie appears to receive mental stimulation from a small black-and-white television set beside her cage showing soap operas all day. Jennie may not understand what she sees, nor sit transfixed; nevertheless, she will on occasion gaze intently at the set. "I feel an important part of my job is to take care of them mentally, as well as physically," says Bond. "If they want to play, I put down whatever I'm doing and indulge them."

At the National Zoo the daily responsibility for the animal is, literally, in the hands of the keepers. Deceptively simple to many, an animal keeper's job requires strenuous work, alertness, intuition, and a certain stoic dedication. As Art Cooper, a lion house keeper since 1966, characterizes it, "I put the animals first in everything I do. They depend on me. If I don't think about them first, I'm not doing my job."

Keepers attempt to make captivity more enjoyable for the animals by providing relief from inactivity. Although an animal's basic needs are met—it is fed, sheltered, and protected from predators—without the stimulation of recreational pursuits the animals can become bored and lazy. Inactivity can lead to serious problems, such as engaging in ster-

In winter, elephants must be hosed down for at least 15 minutes a day to wash off the hay and dust they enjoy rolling in. Here Al Perry administers the shower. Come summer, the elephants can soak in their wading pools.

eotyped behavior: some animals pace back and forth nervously, stand for hours and shake their heads, or continuously repeat one activity. In an attempt to keep animals more alert and thereby healthier, some zoos have started training certain captive animals to respond to keeper commands with behavior typical of that which might be displayed in the wild environment.

Operant conditioning of the Zoo's new sea lions and seals has begun in an effort to demonstrate some natural characteristics of the animals. These would include showing how long a sea lion can stay underwater (20 minutes), or having a blindfolded sea lion dive into the pool and locate a sound-wave machine giving off vibrations similar to those a fish makes moving through the water.

Many veteran zoo keepers are skeptical about the idea of training animals on the grounds that it is demeaning to the animal and tends to be anthropomorphic. It is hoped that the training at the National Zoo will, in contrast, highlight the natural behavior of the animals and not show how much a sea lion can seem like a human.

Daryl Boness, curator of mammals, reluctantly agreed to allow the training of the sea lions and seals. He felt this was necessary so that keepers could summon the animals out of the water for medical exams or pool cleaning. "You need training," he says. "Otherwise keepers would stand on the beach and holler for the animals to come in without getting any response. The only way to get some measure of control over them is to train them. This is a case where I modified my attitude about training," he admits.

The first sea lions—five females and two males—arrived at the Zoo in September 1978. From the outset, keepers hand fed them three times a day to record exactly how much they ate, to monitor their appetites for signs of illness, and to begin operant conditioning. The first task was to get an animal's attention and attempt to get it to target on an object, in this instance the keeper's fist.

Whenever the animal looked at the fist, the keeper blew a whistle and gave the sea lion a fish. Once this pattern was established, the keeper would hold out the fist but not blow the whistle until the sea lion came closer. After this new pattern was established, the next fish treat came only when the sea lion actually placed its nose against the keeper's fist. By these "successive approximations," the animal gradually learned the behavior

On shedding and cleaning: sometimes when a snake sheds its skin the eye caps remain and must be removed with forceps. Above opposite, keepers Bala Demeter and "Trooper" Walsh help out with a king cobra and, at left, with a mangrove snake. Opposite below, Demeter coaxes a cobra back into its cage after cleaning, and Walsh, above, escorts a Burmese python out of its cage. With other snakes, the cages are cleaned with occupants present.

sought by the keepers. Now, when the sea lions are to be examined by the veterinarian, blowing the whistle and holding out a fist brings them out of the water in a hurry.

Boness, who plans to do detailed research into the social behavior, reproductive behavior, and reproductive physiology of the sea lions and seals, is still mildly uncertain whether the training will alter the animals' natural behavior.

"I don't know how much effect the training will have on my research plans. Certainly monitoring hormone levels in the blood should be much easier because the seals will come out of the pool on cue and allow someone to take a blood sample."

One of the most persuasive arguments against training at zoos concerns imprinting, a term given meaning by Konrad Z. Lorenz, the Austrian ethologist. Imprinting is a learning process that occurs early in the life of many social animals, whereby a behavior pattern is established through association with a parent or other role model. For example, Lorenz showed that in the first few hours of its life, a gosling will fixate on whatever moves nearby and develop a strong attachment for that object. Ordinarily, that object is the mother goose, and the gosling will follow it to the ends of the earth. But one day, Lorenz removed the mother immediately after a gosling hatched and made certain that he, Lorenz, was the only object in sight. After an hour or two, it was perfectly clear to the gosling that Konrad Lorenz was its mother.

Although imprinting is quite different in mammals than it is in birds, it is not altogether infrequent for young zoo animals to be imprinted on keepers rather than on a parent or other member of their species. The imprinting thus established may even endure through adulthood and disrupt a planned breeding program. One classic case involved Chi-Chi, a female giant panda at the London zoo flown to Russia in March 1966 to meet and perhaps to mate with An-An, the Moscow zoo's male giant panda.

Nine years old at the time, Chi-Chi had spent the last seven years alone at the London zoo, attentively tended by her human keeper. After six months of acclimatization to Russia, the two pandas were put together for mating. Although in estrus, Chi-Chi ignored the advances of An-An and instead presented herself in the mating posture on several occasions to keepers and other human observers. Chi-Chi identified with humans, not pandas.

Knowledge of Chi-Chi's imprinting led the National Zoo to locate its two pandas next to one another, although in separate cages since they are solitary animals in the wild. The Zoo also decided to rotate keepers so neither panda would develop an attachment to a specific keeper. Put together during mating season, the rest of the year the pandas have only visual, auditory, and olfactory contact through a circle of wire mesh in the wooden fence separating their outdoor yards.

In caring for captive animals, keepers and curators pay close attention to a wide array of environmental requirements, trying to piece together all the fragments of information so that the animal will remain in good health and reproduce. The final element in one of these environmental jigsaw puzzles might well be something as mundane as cage temperature, diet, or cage space. At the National Zoo, keepers, with curatorial supervision, are encouraged to search out the missing pieces.

Keepers' knowledge of the animals' individual behavior patterns and feeding habits helps them solve puzzles related to breeding. Louis Walsh attacked the problem of breeding emerald tree boas in captivity by designing an elaborate exhibit that imitated the 12 hours of daylight in the snake's natural habitat. He kept the humidity as high as that in the Amazonian rain forests and permitted a temperature fluctuation of 26 degrees in a 24-hour period to stimulate the snake to breed. The result was the birth of six live young—one of the first captive breedings of an emerald tree boa. Keeper Walsh successfully bred green tree pythons at his home several years ago, only the second clutch of this species to be bred in captivity in the United States.

William S. Peratino, formerly a keeper at the Bird House, was concerned about the Zoo's nectar-eating birds. Many had never produced offspring, and he suspected that their diet of water, granulated sugar, and a commercial protein supplement was producing a rush of energy, but no real food value. He formulated a new food, a combination of water, honey, commercial protein supplement, hydrolized collagen (connective tissue between muscle and bone already broken down for consumption), wheat germ oil and carrot oil, a water-soluble vitamin supplement for birds, and a commercial cod-liver oil supplement which provides birds in captivity that are not exposed to sunlight with a source of Vitamin D3. After several months on Peratino's health food diet, offspring from Moluccan red lorries and red-crested cardinals were born at the Zoo for the first time. Peruvian cocks-of-the-rock, among other species, became more resplendent in their scarlet coloration.

Peratino now works directly under the Zoo's veterinarian as the animal keeper in the hospital. A man with the physique of a stevedore, there lurks beneath his bulging muscles a fierce passion and devotion to

A baby short-tailed bat clings to Kathy Wallace's shirt in a display area with a reversed light cycle that holds 30 bats. When the cage is cleaned, opposite, the keeper catches the bats with a net and performs a census to see if any have died.

some of nature's most fragile creatures, the birds. As a youngster, Peratino kept parakeets, cats, eels, chameleons, and even praying mantises as pets. He takes much of the knowledge gained at the Zoo home with him to his dazzling assortment of 18 resplendent parrots, a collection that includes grand and red-sided eclectus; Moluccan, umbrella, citron, and lesser sulphur-crested cockatoos; military and blue and gold macaws, and African gray parrots. The birds, worth thousands of dollars, live behind locked steel doors, further protected by an electronic security system.

"You don't keep birds, they keep you," says Peratino. A food enthusiast, he scours grocery stores to buy pomegranates, coconuts, fresh berries, and other seasonal foods which may help stimulate breeding. The Zoo, because it must buy in bulk and fresh food

Injured when attacked by another spider monkey, young Josh had to be hand reared, a task which fell to keeper Sonny Stroman. Josh is fine now.

spoils easily, rarely indulges in the luxury of buying such delicacies for its birds.

*   *   *

Curators oversee all research projects carried out in their respective areas of the Zoo. The classic keeper study involves some aspects of exotic-animal husbandry, but theoretical research is attracting more and more keepers. The degree of curatorial involvement in these studies, like the division of labor in general between keeper and curator, depends on several factors, including the needs of the animals in a particular unit, the initiative of the individual keepers, and the individual curator's beliefs about keeper research projects generally.

Each curator carefully establishes his own animal-care policy with his keeper-leaders. While some curators then rely heavily on these leaders to see that policy is carried out on a day-to-day basis, others feel less comfortable about assigning such a management role. Similarly, some curators consider keepers the real experts in managing animals and allow them considerable leeway in caring for their charges, while other curators supervise as closely as possible all aspects of animal care. In either case, curators communicate several times a day with each keeper, checking data and compiling accurate records of animal activities.

Boness has confidently relied on his keeper-leaders to care for the lions, tigers, and bears in his unit. Since he came to the Zoo in the summer of 1978, he has necessarily had to

devote much of his time to the development of Beaver Valley, the Zoo's elaborate new aquatic exhibit which opened in the spring of 1979. Also involved with setting up breeding programs of both sea lions and grey seals, Boness feels that Beaver Valley's design, with its rocky beach or reef area, closely approximates a rookery in the wild and will therefore accommodate aggressive behavior between males and females.

While keeper input into animal care generally begins after an animal has arrived at the Zoo, curators must research potential Zoo animals beforehand, seeking to balance a species' exhibit value against any difficulties that might arise in caring for or attempting to breed it. For instance, several curators and many other people at the Zoo pooled their expertise to create Beaver Valley, which exhibits—along with the California sea lions and grey seals—North American beaver, river otters, timber wolves, and South American bush dogs. Each curator researched a different species, ensuring that the exhibit would meet the animals' needs.

For example, because river otters require both quiet and regulated temperatures for breeding, curators designed a special room with partitions that can convert into two or three separate otter dens. Furthermore, rubber rimming on the edges of the entrances allows the otter to squeeze itself dry as it enters. Otters depend on their fur for insulation. If the outer layer fails to dry properly, moisture seeps through to the inner hair and the animals can easily die from hypothermia.

In the beaver yard, a concrete barrier with small twigs on it separates upper and lower pools of water, producing the sound of rushing water which curators hope will in turn trigger the beavers' urge to build a dam. Metal pipes sunk into the ground in the enclosure are periodically filled with freshly cut trees for the beavers to gnaw on, and Zoo officials hope they will use the debris to construct dams. In the wild, beaver dams produce enough water backup to keep the entrance to the animals' lodge submerged, thus reducing its vulnerability to predators. Should the animals prove too successful in their dam building, drain basins can handle water overflow, and keepers can occasionally knock down portions of the dams.

Another responsibility of curators is to maintain close and constant contact with the Offices of Animal Health, Education and Information, and Graphics and Exhibits. To better educate the public, Dale Marcellini, curator of reptiles, coordinates curatorial responsibilities with the exhibits staff. Curators decide what pertinent biological information to present the Education and Information Office, which then writes the message for the sign. After further curatorial verification, it is sent to Graphics and Exhibits to be put into final form.

There is no typical exhibit sign. Each animal has an identification sign with such standard material as its common and scientific names; a range map and description of its natural habitat; its diet in the wild; reproductive habits; the number of young born each year; and a statement about its social structure. The curators then seek to illuminate other aspects of the animal with a "key" sign that generally considers evolution in describing the adaptive significance of, say, specific behavior or morphology. One interesting sign with accompanying photographs compares the solitary habit of the Bengal tiger with the social habit of the lion.

In Beaver Valley, the beaver exhibit provides two keys, one a schematic description of different types of beaver lodges and their function, the other both a schematic drawing of how a beaver dam is built and a three-dimensional fiber-glass beaver skull with text on the morphology of beaver teeth.

Both the sea lion and the grey seal exhibits have prominent three-dimensional models of animals' communication patterns during breeding season. In each case, a cutaway of a breeding beach includes realistic animal sculptures in various threat postures, with accompanying text on the function of vocalizations. The Zoo hopes to add an auditory unit that would offer the public a tape of sea lion and seal vocalizations augmented by a discussion of them.

Keepers and curators, who comprise most of the Office of Animal Management, exemplify the closely knit and interrelated nature of Zoo operations. Modern-day shepherds of an ever-increasing number of exotic animals, some of which no longer exist in the wild, they devote themselves to every aspect of their charges. In General Curator Jaren Horsley's words, "We want the public to feel that they have seen something beautiful, that they have been informed, that they liked what they saw, that they want to come back again and bring their friends to share this experience." □

Keeper Jim Jones and his charge, Arusha, one of the Zoo's most successful breeding hippos. With her mate, Joe Smith, she has produced 16 offspring since her arrival here in 1955.

FEEDING TIME

The foods eaten by animals in the Zoo are carefully chosen by the curator of each division. He makes his decision based on information collected by observers in the field, research, and zoo experience over the years. Sometimes not much is known about an animal's requirements or habits, and a curator must just do his best. He decides the diets and determines how the food will be prepared: whether to be left whole or cut into chunks, slices, or small bits. Animals may have different needs depending on how they pick up their food. In consultation with the veterinarian and nutritionist, the curator also decides what food supplements, vitamins, and minerals are needed by each animal during different periods of its life.

Nutrition is considered so important by the Zoo that a full-time nutritionist, Olav Oftedal, has recently been hired to help ensure that the animals receive balanced diets.

Every 12 months the commissary prepares a grocery list for the upcoming fiscal year. Like everyone, they begin with the basics: 55,000 pounds of meat and 10,000 pounds of sweet potatoes. They add the staples—200

Keeper Chris Mercer serving up a banana treat. The fare for marmosets, below, features milk, a meat mix, crickets, carrots, and chopped kale. Some zoo animals, like the snake, center, require rodents for food. White rats, far right, raised for this purpose, are required to be humanely killed and frozen before being consumed.

tons of hay and 220 tons of grain. Then the list is garnished with little things that mean a lot when preparing food—a half-million maggots and a million crickets. When the list is finished, the cost is estimated for the upcoming budget. It was $250,000 this past year, which isn't bad when you consider that it feeds 2,600 animals for an entire year. Some, like the elephants, can really put it away—150 pounds of grain, grass, and hay a day. And the pandas eat more than 100 pounds of bamboo a day—much of it donated by Washington residents. Yet a baby lizard's entire day's diet may consist of an occasional maggot.

Night crawlers, mealworms, and maggots are surprisingly easy to obtain. But locating peas in the pod all year round and fresh sugar cane presents a challenge to Moses Benson, commissary manager.

The food most relished by many of the Zoo's animals would likely be found in a crack in the kitchen wall. Mice and rats are provided for many of the small carnivorous mammals, birds of prey, reptiles, and even some amphibians. About 96,000 are consumed each year.

A relatively new development in feeding captive animals has simplified zoo shopping greatly. It is now possible to buy specially formulated, economical diets for many of the exotic animals. For example, commercially prepared feline diets with vitamin supplements cost about half as much per pound as the slab horsemeat they replaced. And because of their excellent nutritional balance, smaller portions meet the animals' require-

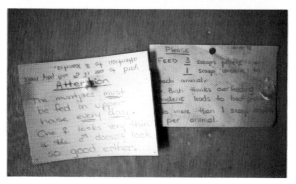

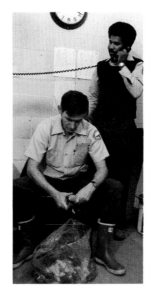

The panda nibbles on bamboo, its preferred food, while, directly below, a keeper trims bamboo before serving it up. Notes indicate muntjac diet. At opposite left, a keeper feeds a tortoise its daily salad, mostly fruits and vegetables. An omnivorous bear noshes, top. Frozen fish are included in its diet. Center, a vitamin pill is inserted before feeding. Meat portions are weighed, above left, while, top right, a commissary worker performs "KP duty." Above, a tray of hydroponically grown oat grass is ready for herbivores.

ments. This is why the Zoo implores its visitors, through educational signs, not to feed the animals.

The commissary is cost-conscious. To beat rising costs, the Zoo grows oat grass hydroponically (in water rather than in soil). If handled correctly, plants grow very quickly. In only eight days the commissary turns oat seed into a luscious, 5-inch-tall carpet of green grass rich in moisture and food value. The hydroponic grass is twice the weight of the original grain and the animals seem to love all of it—sprouts, seeds, and roots.

The next time you are in the Zoo and watch the keepers feed 100 pounds of sea trout to the polar bears or see a hoopoe gobble up a mealworm, you'll realize what's involved in providing suitable diets for the Zoo's large and varied collection of animals. For the eight men who work in the National Zoo's commissary, running a restaurant would be duck soup! □

A tiger receiving its daily meat supply. Giraffes get herbivore pellets, alfalfa, timothy hay, and oat grass. What could be more appropriate for the chimp than a banana? The tawny frogmouth, below right, about to gobble a mouse.

NEAT DUTY

A neat place for noise freaks in the nation's capital is a public park next to National Airport. When the big jets take off just above your head your fillings vibrate, your innards rattle. A better place (except it's not public) is the innards of the hill in Rock Creek Park upon whose grassy swards the National Zoo's big cats loll. Inside that hill in the mornings, keeper Art Cooper wheels big chunks of raw meat along a corridor past the cages where the lions spend the night. This excites the lions. They growl and they roar. The innards of the hill reverberate, the walls amplifying the unholy noise into the most terrifying thunder anyone has ever heard. It is, remember, lions doing this. About 10 lions. And they're on the other side of what all of a sudden seems like some pretty insubstantial mesh. Airplanes have nothing on lions.

Art Cooper is immune to the lions' din. You realize that if he ever felt, as you do, a bit like the Christians did in the Coliseum, he doesn't any more. A big man, no, an enormous man, he exudes calm. Just the kind of man you'd like to have keeping track of nearby lions.

After a stint in the military, Cooper worked for the postal service but "couldn't stand all those people complaining, talking at me all the time. Besides, I wanted to work outdoors." After a while at Baltimore's zoo taking care of bears and big cats, he came to the National Zoo in 1966. Two years later he moved to the lion house and he's been there, just where he wants to be, ever since (Indeed, he seems reluctant to take much leave, even to go fishing, and like other keepers he is inclined to show up at the Zoo in civvies on his days off.)

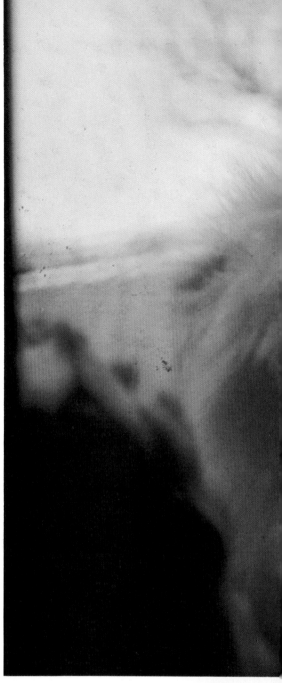

Keeper Art Cooper has been around big cats long enough not to flinch when Antar, a young male Atlas lion, roars at him through the glass, top. Antar is aggressive and doesn't like people. On the other hand, Jakout, a playful young lioness, right, and Amaziga, center and far right, often come to the glass to watch the people. These lions are offspring of four on loan from the zoo in Rabat, Morocco.

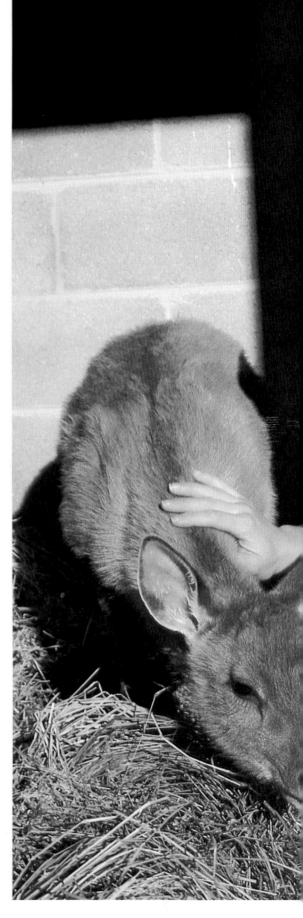

In the keepers' office in the bowels of the hill, Cooper has a photograph of one of his "foster" lion cubs, Amaziga, leading a German shepherd by its leash.

Asked why the big cats attract him, he smiles. "I like their attitude. They're independent. Like me. No one's going to tell them what to do if they don't want to do it. Sometimes one of them doesn't want to come in—or come out—and it'll come up to the door and look at you and then just go away. I'll yell at it a little and if that doesn't work, I just leave it where it is. Most of the time most of 'em do what I say."

Outside, he walks around the big cat exhibit, past the white tigers (the most obstinate of the Zoo's cats, says Cooper), and an orange tiger, lying in the sun, lifts its head.

"That's Marvin. Real name is Marvina but they thought she was a male when she was born. I still call her Marvin. I hand raised her. Hey, Marvin."

"It kind of teed me off," he says, "when Marvin got old and started in to not doing what I asked her to do. But that's cats for you. Independent."

Marvin watched the big man until he was out of sight, then went back to sleep.

If you meander from the lions' domain up the western slope of Rock Creek Park past the pandas' quarters, you will find yourself in one of the quietest parts of the Zoo, loosely known as "the deer area." About the only sound is the swish of traffic on Connecticut Avenue. And very likely you will encounter a quiet young woman in a keeper's uniform striding here and there between the wooded paddocks where Eld's deer, Père David's deer, sable antelope, reindeer, and bongos lead their apparently placid lives.

The young keeper is Barbara Gatzke, a native of the city, who attended the University of Maryland but left to work in an agricultural research station in nearby Beltsville. She wanted to get enough working experience with animals to be able to seek a career in veterinary medicine. She thought zoos were bad news—all those caged animals—but, encouraged by a friend, she applied for a job in the National Zoo without much enthusiasm. Months later, when the Zoo called with a job, she accepted it, still with reservations. She worked here and there, her misgivings about animals in cages falling like leaves. Then she was assigned to the deer and delicate hoofed stock areas and has been happy ever since.

Hoofed stock keeper Barbara Gatzke pats Sammy, an Eld's deer, at left. Against the urban backdrop, top, she feeds hydroponic grass to the Père David's deer, which are often joined in the feast by a free-ranging peacock. Above, Gatzke turns, startled, when an aggressive and ill-tempered sable antelope bull named Himo slams his horns into the bars of his compound. The bull must be locked in his feeding stall when his area is to be cleaned but, a crafty beast, he sometimes escapes this daily capture.

"I like being outdoors," she says. A lot of keepers aren't all that entranced with handling the deer—"some don't like walking up and down the hills"—but Gatzke has a lot of energy and an obvious affection for her charges. And respect. She knows just what a respectful distance means to a male Eld's deer. There is a big male sable antelope named Himo who vigorously butts his enclosure walls when she comes near. "I still don't really trust that fence," she says, only half joking. A sable antelope is a large animal—nearly the size of a small horse—and if aroused (which Himo seems perpetually to be) is highly dangerous.

"Some of these animals are *really* wild," says Gatzke. "It makes it hard to get them when you need to. We've begun to hand raise some of the young. It makes them easier to handle. They aren't tamed. They know they're deer, not humans, but it's safer for the animals. They can hurt themselves if they panic when they've got to be handled." A young Eld's deer named Sammy which Gatzke hand reared seems to know it's a deer, but comes up to her with all the reserve of a friendly puppy when she's on her rounds.

Gatzke is a keeper-leader, not only for the delicate hoofed stock and deer but for the pandas down the hill. That means she must be sure that all the keepers' chores are done. It also means that she must be on hand when any of her animals is to be treated by a vet, moved, or whatnot—even when the gardening staff comes to trim branches in the paddocks. It makes for long hours but that's okay with Gatzke. "I really like to be involved when the vets are here, to see what goes on. I like to know everything that happens to these animals," she says.

Her favorites are the reindeer: those slightly goofy looking beasts from Scandinavia, regarded with some distaste by the other deer keepers since they are more of a problem in the stall-cleaning department. When she cleans their stall, they wander in and out and watch carefully, sometimes getting in the way like children. "It's nice having them around," says Gatzke. "It's not like you're just up here by yourself cleaning cages."

That chore done, Gatzke strides out into the sun and heads down the path to another paddock, for another chore on the hill where the deer live.

"I really love it up here," she says to no one in particular, and you begin to think you know what she means.   □

A greased pig has nothing on a feisty dorcas gazelle. Periodically these magnificent broken-field runners must be rounded up for medical examinations and injections for worms and other parasites. Though it is a bit stressful for the animals, rounding them up and locking them in a restraining cage has been determined to be the best way to immobilize them. The process has also been found stressful to keepers.

IN SICKNESS AND HEALTH

DOCTORING EXOTIC ANIMALS

Thomas Crosby

India, it is thought, became the birthplace of veterinary medicine in 250 B.C. when King Asoka the Great held a convocation that subsequently decreed Buddhism to be the state religion. Simultaneously, he ordered the construction of veterinary hospitals for the treatment and care of all native animals, including elephants, game birds, fish, and domesticated livestock. This potentially bright beginning in the quest for knowledge about animals, including exotics, dimmed after Asoka's death. For the next two thousand years, animal health care was virtually unknown. In the West, the Roman Empire, which slaughtered animals for entertainment rose and fell; the Dark Ages arrived with their anti-science tinge; then came the Reformation and the rebirth of scientific curiosity.

In 1761 the first veterinary college opened in Lyon, France, and 100 years later, during the Civil War, colleges in the United States began offering courses and degrees in veterinary medicine; but study naturally centered on such animals as the horse, dog, cow, and cat. Veterinary curricula were devoid of courses about the care and treatment of exotic animals. Even today, fewer than half of the 22 professional veterinary institutions in this country offer any specialized courses in exotic animal medicine.

Prior to World War II this lack of knowledge and interest in the health needs of exotic animals meant high death rates in U.S. zoos, with the survival of animals depending on the experience of head keepers who learned their medical skills through word of mouth or by trial and error.

During the Zoo's early days, Head Keeper William Blackburne used remedies acquired during his circus years as well as from keepers at other zoos. To treat a tiger with sarcoptic mange (caused by tiny mites burrowing into the skin), Blackburne once climbed on top of the cat's cage and poured half a bucketful of sulfur and oil on the animal. When the same tiger had indigestion, Blackburne, again atop the cage, used a carriage whip to tickle its nose. The huge cat roared, and Blackburne poured a quart of castor oil into its gaping jaws. It was rudimentary, hit-and-miss medicine, to be sure.

The treatment of Buster, a 1,160-pound Alaskan Peninsula bear who could scarcely walk because of painful corns on his paws, called for only a little more sophistication. Cotton soaked with two pounds of ether was held under the bear's nose. When he became groggy, ropes were used to pull him to the cage bars where the two large corns on each forefoot were surgically removed and the feet bandaged by a veterinarian from the U.S. Department of Agriculture's Bureau of Animal Industry. The ether took full effect after the operation, and the bear slept for several days. But he never again suffered from corns.

Today, as in the past, veterinarians and pathologists trained traditionally in the physiology and anatomy of domestic animals face a different set of problems when it comes to exotics. For example, maned wolves are in the same taxonomic family as the dog, but these Brazilian canids have short gastrointestinal tracts and appear to process food much more rapidly than do dogs. Hippopotamuses and pigs share taxonomic relationships, but the hippo usually has only one offspring a year while a sow may have 15 piglets in a litter. Chickens—the only bird studied in the typical education of a veterinarian—have little in common with fish-eating bald eagles, penguins that can contract malaria, or large flightless birds like emus or ostriches. Reptiles and amphibians receive even less attention in veterinary schools.

Exotic animal medicine has always been the stepchild of regular veterinary practice, partly because most zoos could not afford to hire full-time staff veterinarians in the past and partly because zoo work carried little professional prestige. The National Zoo did not have a staff veterinarian in its early years (the first was hired in 1954). For complicated medical treatments or necropsies, the Zoo re-lied on the good will and assistance of government agencies like the Bureau of Animal Industry or the Armed Forces Institute of Pathology. In addition, while textbooks abound on the medical treatment of cows, dogs, cats, horses, pigs, chickens, sheep, and goats, few such texts deal comprehensively with tigers, elephants, sable antelope, cheetahs, bush dogs, rhinoceroses, tapirs, and bald eagles. In 1923 H. Fox published one of the first English-language, exotic-animal medical textbooks, *Diseases of Captive Wild Mammals and Birds*. Another 55 years passed before an updated medical textbook useful primarily to zoos, Dr. Murray Fowler's *Zoos and Wild Animal Medicine*, appeared.

The Bronx zoo gets credit for hiring the first veterinarian in 1901, followed by the San Diego Zoo in 1929. But despite the obvious advantage of having a resident animal doctor, other zoos were slow to jump on the bandwagon. In 1966 only nine U.S. zoos employed full-time veterinarians. But late in the 1960s and early 1970s, veterinary medicine —along with animal conservation and ecologic concern—rose in popularity as a profession. Half of the 60 major North American zoos had a staff veterinarian by 1978. Moreover, the volume of applicants to veterinary schools exceeded the competition for entrance into some human medical schools.

Theodore H. Reed, who was hired as the National Zoo's second clinical veterinarian in 1955 (the first resigned after eight months), remembers how it was:

"When I first came here the Zoo's main

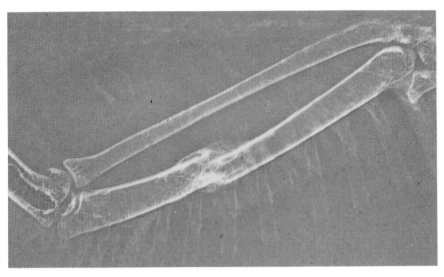

An X-ray reveals a broken ulna. Ordinarily, animals are X-rayed only during routine physicals.

Veterinarian Mitchell Bush and Jandel Allen, a summer intern, prepare to trap pigeons for research at the Zoo and other institutions.

defense against disease was scrupulous cleanliness—hot water, soap, and pine oil. There was no penicillin, no safe anesthetics, and no money to buy drugs. I had to get drugs by begging free samples from drug salesmen. After awhile, they stopped coming by because I rarely bought anything. If I needed a drug in a hurry, I would go to the drugstore across the street from the Zoo and buy it with my own money."

Fifteen months after being hired, Dr. Reed became the Zoo's acting director, and the veterinarian who had had to scrimp and save to get drugs and money to treat animals began using his influence to place greater emphasis on the medical side of zoo-keeping. By the early 1970s the National Zoo's animal health program was recognized as among the best in the United States.

The modern cornerstone of the Zoo's health care is a highly sophisticated preventive medicine program that seeks, by prudent procedures, to keep the animals from becoming sick. Susceptibility in certain species to specific diseases—and the hurdles that must be overcome in curing any exotic animal disease—have prompted a program of

regular vaccinations, periodic analysis of animal feces, annual tuberculin tests, quarantine of newly arrived animals, and blood tests whenever an animal receives medical treatment.

Illness in domestic animals, especially pets, often can be easily detected. Exotic animals, on the other hand, tend to mask any signs of infection or debility, for in the wild their survival may depend on their ability to hoodwink predators into perceiving that all is well. As a result of this instinctive survival technique, wild animals in captivity may be close to death by the time zoo keepers or veterinarians spot a behavioral quirk brought on by illness or injury—adding incentive for zoos to keep animals from becoming sick in the first place.

But it isn't, and wasn't, easy. On one occasion, before the turn of the century, Lt. Robert Edwin Peary, the discoverer of the North Pole, borrowed back two Eskimo dogs he had loaned the Zoo. When he returned them, one of the dogs had distemper, which quickly spread and killed many of the Zoo's dogs, wolves, and foxes. Several outbreaks occurred in years following but not since the early 1960s, when the Zoo embarked on a preventive vaccination program.

Regular vaccinations against feline distemper are given to the National Zoo's tigers, Geoffrey cats, lions, and other cats, while maned wolves, bush dogs, hyenas, and other members of the dog family receive vaccinations against canine distemper. Numerous animals receive vaccinations against both types, among them fur-bearing animals such as zorillas, badgers, ferrets, grisons, and carnivorous small mammals such as binturongs, civets, and mongooses. Newborn animals receive four to five vaccinations, and newly arrived animals are vaccinated during their quarantine period. All the animals receive yearly boosters.

Tuberculosis, a highly contagious disease, is as dangerous as distemper and can afflict birds, reptiles, hoofed stock and other mammals, attacking bones, intestines, skin, and lymph nodes. Annual tuberculin tests are given the Zoo's primates, a process that requires, first, immobilization, and then injection of an extract of the TB organisms—tuberculin—into the eyelid to determine the presence of TB bacteria. If the lid swells, it indicates the animal has been exposed to such bacteria, although the animal may not actually have developed a full-blown case of

Dr. Bush reaches for a captured pigeon. Some-times troublesome to Zoo birds, these local vis- **itors are regularly monitored to see if they carry avian diseases. Soaring flight cage is seen at rear.**

tuberculosis. The injection is made in the eyelid so that the reaction can be observed at a distance.

Five of the National Zoo's eight great apes displayed positive reactions to tuberculin injection in 1968. As a result, their exhibit was closed to the public for three months be-cause of the possibility of tuberculosis trans-ference from primates to humans (this in spite of the fact that humans are more likely to infect other mammals). The apes were put through numerous TB tests, and it was finally determined that they had only an allergic reaction to the tuberculin.

Another important form of preventive medicine involves the periodic analysis of animal feces to determine the presence of internal parasites, usually worms, which can weaken an animal's ability to fight off disease or injury. No zoo animal is safe from them.

Some of the most troublesome are round-worms and stomach worms, which attack the digestive tract in snakes; gape-worms that attach to the trachea in birds; and several varieties of worms that attack mammalian gastrointestinal tracts. Hoofed stock confined to small pastures are susceptible to parasitic diseases, and especially to reinfestation.

The dorcas gazelle herd, for example, suf-fers from parasites because their paddock isn't large enough for them to avoid coming into contact with their own fecal matter—a problem that rarely occurs in the wild, where there is abundant open space. Parasitic eggs deposited on the ground in the gazelle yard remain until the grazing animals eat the grass and ingest the eggs. These then hatch in the gastrointestinal tract and develop into mature parasites. The eggs produced by the parasites are passed through the animal and deposited

Keeper Al Perry inspecting the nails of Shanti, an Asiatic elephant. In the wild, rocky terrain serves to abrade nails. At the Zoo, however, periodic pedicures with a rasp are a necessity.

on the ground, completing the cycle. "We can keep the parasite load under control by constant treatment, but we can't cure them," says Mitchell Bush, chief veterinarian.

Where distemper vaccinations and tuberculin testing require injections, preventive worming is done comparatively simply by placing antiworm drug powders on the animal's food. A few drugs come in various flavors, such as banana, liver, or cherry, and the proper flavor must be found for certain picky eaters.

Zoo veterinarians begrudgingly accept parasites as an ineradicable enemy; other implacable foes are the local pests which infest zoos. Pigeons, rats, mice, foxes, raccoons, squirrels, possums, dogs—even domestic cats—all pose a threat as they roam the Zoo, often mingling with exotic animals, stealing food, or, in the case of the cats and raccoons, stalking and killing rare birds. Any of these unofficial interlopers could carry an infectious disease, but they cannot be eliminated in the usual manner. Poison used to kill a mouse or pigeon threatens the Zoo's carnivorous animals because they might devour the toxic remains.

This has led Zoo employees to jokingly call the Panda House a "half-million-dollar mouse house" because visitors, especially young children, appear as fascinated with the mice scurrying over Ling-Ling's or Hsing-Hsing's rice and carrots, as with the world-famous pandas themselves. Poisoning the mice poses a danger to the pandas, who occasionally catch and devour the rodents. As a result, both metal and wooden spring traps baited with cheese are scattered around the interior of the Panda House, out of the way of the pandas. The mice, however, continue to show more interest in the panda food, seldom being lured by the scent of cheese.

All animals arriving at the Zoo must undergo quarantine—another form of precautionary medicine—to prevent the possible introduction of a new disease into the collection. Quarantine provides the Zoo's Office of Animal Health a chance to examine the animal for parasites, take X-rays, and obtain blood samples. If the animal proves healthy, the data collected can be used as a standard against which to evaluate the animal if it later appears ill.

Before the Zoo's new quarantine building

opened in 1978, animals were confined in cages in the hospital and research building, often uncomfortably close to sick and recuperating animals. Divided into three parts, the new edifice allows segregation of various species and markedly reduces the chances of contagion. Three indoor stalls—one padded for skittish animals—and two outdoor stalls are reserved for hoofed stock and large mammals. Two identical but separate interior rooms each contain five small cages and one large cage built into the wall, plus a portable chimpanzee cage. Anyone entering these two rooms must don rubber boots and overalls and step in a germicidal solution to prevent the transmission of bacteria from one room to another or into the Zoo proper.

The National Zoo's prophylactic medicine program—vaccinations, fecal analysis, tuberculosis testing, pest control, and quarantine—is among the most comprehensive and systematic of any U.S. zoo. Yet captive exotic animals living in a foreign climate and eating substitute foods still become sick. Being a Zoo veterinarian means living with a constantly changing schedule because of emergencies—some of which require only a minute or two of visual observation and others which demand hours of delicate surgery. The availability of the veterinarian is crucial; Mitch Bush, who became the Zoo's vet in 1974, works seven days a week and is on call 24 hours a day.

Morning rounds include a visit to all the animal areas and checking with keepers about behavioral and physical deviations. In the Zoo's vigilance with respect to disease, the keepers act as an early warning system. When something goes awry with an animal—a sudden loss of appetite, unexplained sluggishness, or an overnight quarrel between cage mates that has left one animal injured—it is the keeper's responsibility to report it. Dr. Bush cannot always make visual inspections himself because many of the animals remember unpleasant encounters with him—either an immobilizing injection or a wrestling match while the animal was restrained for treatment.

"Some of the gorillas can spot me in a crowd of 200 people," says Bush. When he passes their cages, the great apes will throw feces, bound about their cages in a threatening manner, or occasionally cower in a corner, making themselves a poor target in case the veterinarian has come to shoot them with the immobilizing dart gun.

An African lion from a Largo, Maryland, wild animal park, snarling its discontent. The lion wears a fiber-glass cast originally designed for human use.

Maxine, a white-cheeked gibbon with a recurring leg problem, feared Bush for all the times he anesthetized her or worked on her leg while someone else restrained her. When checking on Maxine's progress—she frequently reopened the wound herself—Bush would stay away from Maxine's outdoor cage and Suzanne Kennedy, a veterinary intern, approached instead. Maxine's painful memories didn't include Dr. Kennedy, and the gibbon would even come to the bars and allow her to examine the injured leg.

Not all animals, of course, exhibit such fear of the veterinarian. Clinton W. Gray, Bush's predecessor, once shot an immobilizing dart into Archie, a male orangutan. The surprised animal, who had a placid and trusting personality, removed the dart, ambled over to the cage bars, and handed it back to the startled Dr. Gray.

Once a determination is made that an animal needs to be examined for an illness, a carefully balanced process comes into play.

There are risks in catching some birds, such as tinamous, pheasants, and rheas, because they can drop dead from the stress caused by human handling. But failure to check the bird for illness could also mean death, if it has a serious disease. "It's like riding a double-edged sword," says Bush.

Restraining animals, if that becomes necessary, raises special problems with each species. Snakes are usually caught by hand and carried to the hospital in wooden boxes or, if they are huge, heavy constrictors, in plastic garbage cans. Carnivores such as lions and tigers are chased into metal squeeze cages—often forced inside by the threat of a water hose or the noise and foam from a carbon dioxide fire extinguisher. Locked in their barn stalls at night, hoofed stock can be transferred into narrow, portable wooden stalls or, in more dire circumstances, shot with an immobilizing gun. Birds and small monkeys are caught by hand or with cloth nets. Large mammals such as elephants, giraffes, and hippopotamuses present easy targets in their enclosures for immobilizing guns or injection with a pole syringe.

Immobilization decisions entail certain risks because of the lack of specific information on what drug to use and how much. For humans, anesthesiologists calculate body weight, body size, sex, and age to determine the proper dose—one which involves minimal risk to the patient. The veterinarian must prescribe a dose that neither harms the animal during immobilization nor keeps it unconscious too long. Too much anesthesia has proven fatal to elephants because the sheer physical pressure of being supine causes their bodily fluids to slowly seep into their lungs, inducing suffocation. Elephant operations, therefore—say, the removal of an infected tusk—must be precisely timed for completion within two hours so the elephant can be back on its feet before the potential lung problem develops.

For many years zoo veterinarians rendered animals immobile for treatment by using drugs. In general, most of these drugs caused muscle paralysis but did not prevent the animal from feeling pain. The only effective drug available prior to the Vietnam War had a serious flaw—the mortality rate of animals injected with it reached 10 percent or greater.

Now most zoos use morphine derivatives which, combined with a tranquilizer, effectively immobilize hoofed stock or other large mammals like elephants, giraffes, and rhinoceroses. The animals go down quickly and seem to suffer few aftereffects. Veterinarians working with the drug have to be wary, however, because it can prove deadly to humans, causing severe respiratory depression if accidentally absorbed into the bloodstream through a cut or the mouth.

One other hurdle must be overcome after a drug is selected—determining the proper dosage. While 1.5 milligrams of a certain drug will immobilize a 4,000-pound rhinoceros, a 200-pound white-tailed deer might require five times as much. Different species react differently to the same drug, reflecting the largely unknown physiology of exotic animals. Even similar species can have different responses. A 900-pound polar bear usually becomes unconscious with one milligram of a drug called M-99, while a 200-pound grizzly requires six milligrams. Veterinarians are baffled by this fluctuation.

Equally baffling is the fact that dosages which work well in one zoo collection do not work exactly the same way in another—possibly because of different diets, different climates and altitudes, or even different blood lines—forcing individual zoos to work out the exact dosages for their animals by trial and error.

A pioneering science still in its infancy, zoological medicine has made tremendous strides since the discovery in the mid-1960s of the immobilizing gun, first used extensively on exotic animals by the National Zoo. Previously, many animals, such as feisty hoofed stock or belligerent gorillas, could not be examined closely without running a considerable risk of injury in the process of restraining them.

Despite its diagnostic value, Bush keeps usage of the immobilizing gun to a minimum, partly because of the psychological trauma it causes the great apes, the physical trauma it causes hoofed stock (deep bruises around the dart point), and the danger that something unexpected can go wrong. If an injection must be made, he prefers to use the pole syringe first, if possible.

After immobilization, the problem turns to diagnosis. Bush has pioneered in using X-rays and the laparoscope on exotic animals. Critical information is also provided by blood chemistries, white blood cell counts, urinalysis, bacterial and fungal cultures, pregnancy and other laboratory tests.

The use of X-rays on exotic animals presents a challenge, since there is often no available standard by which to distinguish the abnormal from the normal in these animals. The Zoo, however, has slowly built a radiographic file so that previous X-rays of an animal of the same species can provide clues when examining a new one. Radiographs are used by the Zoo to diagnose acute diseases, to study the disease's effect, to monitor the efficacy of treatment, and to acquire data to be used in distinguishing normal from abnormal. Diagnoses of Zoo animals successfully aided by radiographs include the discovery that the tusk of a 16-year-old African elephant had become infected and had a hollow core; that a female Komodo dragon had a circular mass in her abdomen, later found to be a calcified egg shell; that a bald-headed pigeon with chronic soft tissue swelling around the elbow proved to be suffering from tuberculosis; and that a lame lion cub in a case referred to the Zoo was beginning to suffer decalcification of the bones because of an exclusive diet of horsemeat, whose high phosphorus-calcium ratio disrupts bone metabolism.

Another vital diagnostic tool is the laparoscope, which permits the veterinarian to see an animal's internal organs. It has been used primarily by human doctors for surgery on female reproductive organs and for general diagnostic evaluation of the abdominal cavity. A small stainless steel tube 2 to 10 millimeters in diameter and between 15 and 35 millimeters long, it contains a series of up to 30 telescopic lenses. When the tube is inserted through a small incision, after the abdomen has been slightly inflated with air to give the vet some room for his probes, the lenses allow a 180-degree view of the internal organs with extensive depth of vision. Accessory instruments can be used to take a biopsy of a liver or kidney for laboratory analysis. The laparoscope has been particularly helpful in determining sex of birds. Since many birds do not display sexual dimorphism (differences in size or plumage) until a certain age, even experienced bird keepers are unable to definitively determine sex until maturity. The laparoscope, however, makes this task easy, allowing early pairing of males and females.

In addition to sexing birds, laparoscopy aids in vasectomies on animals like the crab-eating foxes, lions, and tigers, and permits photographs to be made of internal organs. At the National Zoo, where hundreds of laparoscopic examinations have been per-

All Zoo birds are banded and their bands routinely checked to make certain they don't constrict the bird's movements or dig into its leg.

The webbed foot of an aquatic bird being examined for skin lesions and possible infection. The flaw proved to be only irregular pigmentation.

formed without harm to the animals (one adult female cheetah was examined 15 times in 14 months), laparoscopy has determined which of two female cheetahs was capable of reproduction by monitoring the ovaries in various reproductive phases; helped discover a pelvic adhesion that made a 5-year-old female gorilla a poor breeding prospect; and showed that a female white Bengal tiger had begun ovulating without any contact with a male. Up until this time, tigresses had been thought to be induced ovulators, meaning that only copulation could stimulate ovulation. The discovery of the white Bengal tigress' spontaneous ovulation is an isolated observation to be sure, but it has far-ranging implications and may prove extremely relevant in establishing rational artificial insemination programs for these big cats in zoos.

Because of the evolving nature of veterinary medicine, treatment sometimes can take a unique twist, as in the case of Marvin, a 300-pound Bengal tiger with a 3½-inch lac-

Dr. Bush making a visual check of mother and offspring. Though giraffes occasionally suffer from hoof problems and experience difficult births, in general they thrive in zoos.

eration on her left rear leg. On 12 separate occasions the Zoo veterinarians had placed Marvin (misnamed at birth) in an aluminum alloy squeeze cage, cleaned her wound with disinfectants, and placed swathes of gauze bandages on the leg. After only a few days Marvin would gnaw the bandage off and re-open the wound.

Frustrated by the tiger's behavior, Bush had an idea while putting on the cast for the 13th time. During lunch, members of the hospital staff often visit a nearby Mexican fast-food restaurant. After ordering enchiladas, tortillas, and tostadas to go, lunchers would pick up small plastic cups full of hot sauce and chili peppers. One day, as Marvin lay unconscious, Bush smeared hot sauce and peppers on the big cat's spotless white bandage and added a touch of Tabasco sauce.

After being transported back to the lion and tiger house, the unsuspecting tiger regained consciousness. As keeper Art Cooper watched, she started to lick her gourmet bandage. "You should have seen the expression on her face when she tasted the hot sauce," laughed Cooper, who hand raised Marvin in his Baltimore apartment after she was injured as a cub. "It was just like a human tasting something too hot. She stuck her tongue out and frowned. It was a priceless expression."

For two days Marvin left the smelly bandage alone. But as the potency of the sauce faded, she again gnawed on the cast. Two weeks later the 14th bandage was applied intentionally loosely. However, the wound had surprisingly begun to heal and, when the bandage came off after three days, no new dressing was needed. Six weeks after the hot sauce remedy, Marvin's leg was so improved she was allowed outside. For the first time in 10 months she roamed the grassy, three-tiered tiger exhibit, limping only slightly on her rear leg. Was the sauce the cure? "No, but it helped," says Bush.

Such constant improvisation and imagination are what is needed to cope with the challenge of treating captive wild animals. During his tenure, Bush has grafted bone from a wolf's rib to mend its fractured leg, used a syringe casing to create an artificial leg for a serpent eagle that might have died if it couldn't perch, and placed a cast on the good leg of a lion to make her put weight on a once-injured paw that had healed. The lion had developed the habit of limping, even though it no longer had to.

Carefully documenting his procedures so that other zoo veterinarians can duplicate his methods if faced with similar problems, Bush tries to disseminate his findings through the publication of numerous technical papers based on his experiences.

Aiding Bush in the quest for answers about exotic animal medicine is Richard J. Montali, the Zoo's pathologist, who makes sure a necropsy is performed after the death of every animal—from a day-old baby chick to a 50-year-old Siberian crane.

A veterinarian with special training in pathology, Dr. Montali is one of the two full-time veterinary pathologists working in an American zoo (the other one is in San Diego). His scientific detective work often prevents one animal death from quickly multiplying into many. In 1976 Montali dramatically proved to the zoo community the value of dissecting and researching the cause of death in exotic animals.

The Zoo's last anteater died first, followed five days later by the death of a dik-dik, a small African antelope. Montali was unable to pinpoint the cause of death of the anteater, nor did he link the two deaths at first. But the dik-dik, he found, died of yersiniosis—a deadly disease that is often called pseudo-tuberculosis and that can be transmitted between animals and humans. When no other animals became sick, it was felt the disease had been confined to the dik-dik. Two months after the anteater's death, however, a blesbok suddenly died, followed by another blesbok the following day. A third death occurred three days later.

Fearing an epidemic, Montali began intensive scientific search to see if the anteater, dik-dik, and blesbok deaths were related. Representative specimens of all organs were taken, and selected tissue samples stained for microscopic examination. Specimens of lungs, liver, spleen, small intestine, heart blood, and abdominal wall fluid were cultured for bacteria and fungi, with several cultures going to two different laboratories for confirmation of yersiniosis. Because of the possibility the disease may have been brought in by vermin, Zoo personnel trapped four rats and two pigeons. After blood samples were taken, they were euthanized and necropsied, tissue specimens being collected in the process.

Nine days after the first blesbok death the diagnosis was confirmed as yersiniosis, a threat to other animals and humans. Antibiotics were immediately administered to animals exposed to the disease. Keepers in the hoofed stock area were forbidden to visit other areas of the Zoo. All Zoo employees were warned to wash their hands carefully before eating. A concentrated extermination

It is an almost daily task on the part of Zoo staff to examine giraffe hoofs, which can become painfully overgrown or develop cracks. If a crack appears, a line is filed perpendicular to it to disperse stress and prevent further cracking.

program quickly eliminated the suspected disease carriers—wild rodents and pigeons. The Zoo's fourth, and last, blesbok received massive doses of antibiotics. It survived.

"Our biggest concern is an infectious disease that could go through the Zoo and wipe out a lot of animals," says Montali, who also discovered an outbreak of deadly DVE (duck viral enteritis) in the spring of 1975. In the space of less than one month, it killed 27 ducks, including North American black ducks, wood ducks, scaups, shelducks, goldeneye, buffleheads, common mergansers, widgeon, and an Australian gray teal.

Montali's diagnosis, based on necropsies and analysis of tissue samples of liver, spleen, esophagus, cecum, cloaca, and brain, resulted in 800 remaining birds being vaccinated with a modified live-virus vaccine. Zoo officials also realized at the time that if the disease had not been discovered early on, the entire bird collection could have been lost. Like the yersiniosis, the DVE was apparently brought in by nonresidents, this time wild migratory waterfowl which frequently use the open ponds as refueling stops on trips north and south. (What with pinioned wings, Zoo birds do not join the migrations.)

The necropsies take place in a new Pathology Building, a brick-and-stone structure equipped with its own ultraviolet-lighted cooler to keep bacteria from spreading. Outside is an incinerator capable of devouring 175 pounds of flesh and bones an hour without spewing any pollutants—or more impor-

tantly, any infectious organisms—into the air. Everyone leaving the building must step in a germicidal solution to reduce the possible transmission of disease.

In addition to preventing epidemics, Montali's examinations provide vital clues about a deceased animal's adaptation to his captive environment—diet, cage space, medical treatment, even the air the animal breathes.

"The Zoo represents a repository of animals that we can use to monitor the environment," says Montali. "These animals live in the same setting as people—breathe the same air, drink the same water. What affects them, affects us."

By way of example, older animals that die at the Zoo often have large deposits of air pollutants in their lungs, principally carbon and silicone. A few years ago, the Zoo's primates were found to be victims of lead poisoning, having picked lead-based paint flecks from their cage bars and ingested them, eventually exhibiting the same symptoms as children who eat small amounts of lead-based paint. The Zoo immediately adopted regulations forbidding the use of lead-based paint, and no other incidents of such poisoning have occurred since.

Frequently, necropsies reveal a missing ingredient in an animal's diet which calls for vitamin or mineral supplements in the food of living animals. A flock of six brown peli-

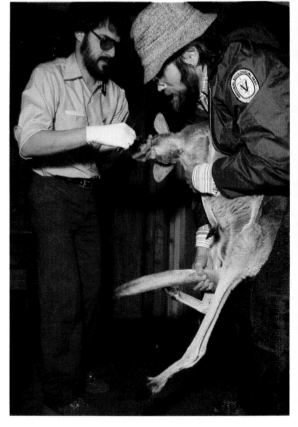

Bush examines a rhino, top, and assists veterinary intern Richard Cambre, above, in flushing an abcess on the jaw of a kangaroo.

cans had once been placed on a diet of frozen smelts. Five of the birds were either found dead or died suddenly while being handled. Necropsies revealed heart and muscle degeneration that appeared to be caused by a vitamin E-selenium deficiency since these elements were not contained in the frozen smelts. A sixth pelican, given vitamin E-selenium and thiamine, recovered.

Representative samples are taken from every organ of a deceased animal—muscles, nerves, heart, lungs, liver, intestines, brain, etc.—sealed in small plastic bags containing preservative fluid, and stored in cardboard boxes in the Pathology Building. Each organ is identified with the animal's accession number—the number given every animal that enters the Zoo. Thus, years after a necropsy it will still be possible for veterinary pathologists to examine the organs of a long-dead animal. New medical discoveries can sometimes turn back the clock and, years after a death, pinpoint its cause.

Approximately 18 percent of the National Zoo's animals die each year—a death rate Montali and Bush feel is comparable to that of any modern urban zoo setting. Every death is included in the statistics, from an aborted fetus to the demise of a 2-minute-old hatchling. In 1977, the Zoo incurred 638 deaths, a figure offset by over 900 births.

"The public image of a pathologist is someone associated with the morbid," says Montali. "But most pathologists are like detectives. The cause of death is a puzzle to solve."

Detailed records of pathological findings and medical histories of every animal in the Zoo are kept by Montali and Bush. An entire file system containing worming history, distemper vaccinations, and tuberculin testing was devised and implemented by keeper William Peratino. A computerized storage and retrieval system stores data collected by Montali on a computer located in the Johns Hopkins Department of Comparative Medicine. This system makes it possible to locate information on cause of death, pathologic diagnoses, organ involvement, age, sex, date of death, and other important data. Another computer system at Johns Hopkins keeps track of over 5,000 color photographs taken of clinical health problems in living and dead animals. The computer systems serve as teaching aids to veterinarians and students, and are similar in format to the International Species Inventory System (ISIS), which at-

A gnu still anesthesized after surgery is weighed, one of the few occasions when weighing is easy.

tempts to keep track of zoo animals around the world.

By amassing such records, the National Zoo hopes to develop standards by which, one day, veterinarians will be able to measure the health of a particular animal. Currently, no one knows the normal temperature of a polar bear or the normal blood pressure of a Barbary ape.

Professional seminars, veterinary journals, an informal long-distance telephone network, year-long training of veterinary interns, and two- to six-week work periods at zoos for veterinary students, all help advance the knowledge of exotic animal medicine.

In his search for answers, Bush never hesitates to raid local hospitals or medical colleges to seek advice or a helping hand from specialists. A veterinary ophthalmologist helped put a synthetic eye in a striped owl; an orthopedic surgeon operated on an orangutan and a Bengal tiger to see if leg joints had been damaged by infection; a parasitologist helped look for parasites in primates; and Bush has received assistance as well from oral surgeons, pediatricians, anesthesiologists, radiologists, and urologists.

"I can get a doctor to look at a sick gorilla quicker than I can get one to look at me," says Bush.

Once the stepchild of veterinary medicine, zoo animal health care has now caught the scientific imagination of the entire medical profession. □

TAKING CARE

At the command "Tail up!" elephants at the National Zoo respond by grabbing a neighbor's tail with a swing of their trunk, lumbering into single file, and waiting for the next order. This kind of line-up is as important for zoo animals as it is for circus elephants, for it is intimately related to the exacting process of caring for animals.

While some may see this roustabout behavior as unnecessarily strict, it actually takes years of experience and education to make the elephants come in from their paddocks and lie down calmly, then endure veterinarians' detailed probing. Many keepers have checked their training skills with colleagues at Busch Gardens, Florida, and elsewhere.

And thus a tradition remains unbroken: the National Zoo's first elephant caretaker and head keeper was William Blackburne, the former Barnum & Bailey "bull man." To maintain the health of the Zoo's original pair of pachyderms, Blackburne would take them down to Rock Creek for exercise and water. This saved the Zoo—then operating under humble conditions—from the expense of installing a main for water, that essential ingredient of animal well-being.

Water remains a vital element in the health and cleanliness of the animals, notably of the Zoo's newest superstars, the seals and sea lions that live in the recently completed pools down in Beaver Valley. Curator Daryl Boness sees marine mammals as a "fresh and tough field for veterinary medicine." The challenge occurs mainly in dealing with skin and eye problems, which are typical in captive marine mammals. When the seals are out of water, keepers look for cloudy areas in the brown eyes and welts on the skin, promptly reporting worrisome signs to the vets.

The somewhat varying symptoms suggest that there may be more than one cause for both eye and skin maladies. Some zoologists and veterinarians believe that both types of problems are by-products of transferring the animals from their native saltwater habitats

Elephants follow zoo rule of health through safety by learning to line up, right, and obey commands of keeper Jim Jones with hook and stool, opposite above. Sea lions respond to whistle blast by nosing Lisa Stevens' friendly fist, opposite below. Keepers watch for possible abrasions or uncharacteristic behavior, opposite right.

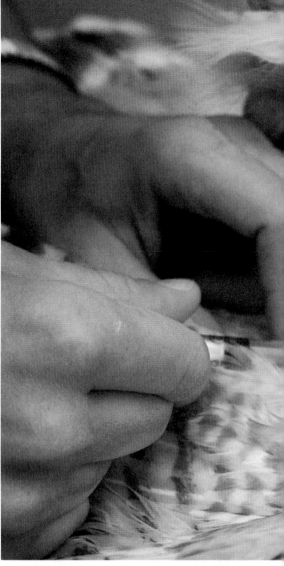

to filtered freshwater. Others believe that these disorders result from the stress of being in a foreign environment, continually on display and removed from natural activities. Proponents of this latter theory often advocate activity training, urging that a busy seal is a healthy seal.

Whether the animal lives in water or on land, zoo keepers take special care with the cleanliness of their charges' environments. Indoor cages are regularly hosed down and may be given a blast of antiseptic if infestation is suspected. Keepers routinely rake and change the sand and gravel in outdoor enclosures. As medical and pharmaceutical knowledge increases, it becomes easier to keep animals healthy in natural settings with soil and living plants, relying less on the easily sterilized concrete and steel floors that were formerly necessary.

"Preventive medicine is the backbone of zoological medicine," states Mitchell Bush, veterinarian-in-charge. This includes quarantine procedures, routine parasite monitoring, vaccination, and tuberculin testing. In 1977 both Dr. Bush and Richard J. Montali, head of the Office of Pathology, noted the lower incidence of avian tuberculosis as a major changing trend, with the incidence about half that of each of the previous two years.

But in spite of the many precautions, zoo animals are susceptible to some of the same

Veterinarian Richard Cambre examines Josh, a spider monkey, right, which injured leg in accident and behaves much like a scared baby (which it is). Dr. Cambre takes monkey's blood, opposite, for analysis via computer.

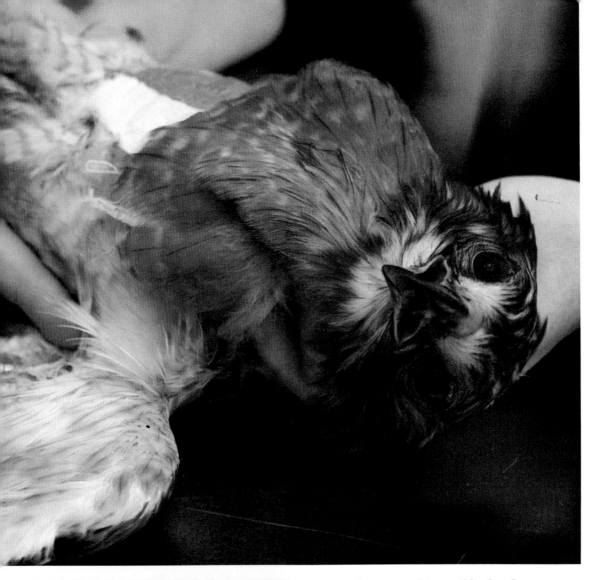

Zoo vets also respond to neighborhood emergencies, as when ornithologists brought in red-shouldered hawk with broken wing, above. Blood tests on such visitors gauge health of wild creatures with which zoo animals might have contact.

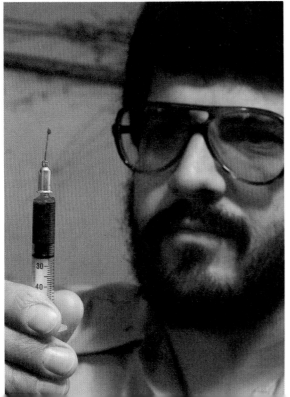

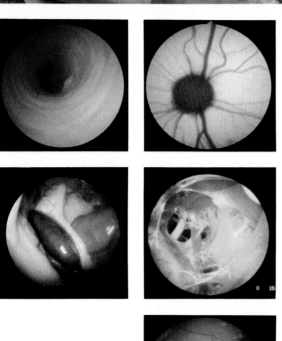

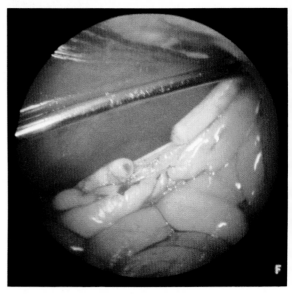

Into the abdomen of an anesthetized cheetah, Mitchell Bush inserts a laparoscope, top. Next the surgeon's wand probes internal organs, above; photo was snapped within the animal by means of fiber optics connected to outside camera. Laparoscopic views at left record inner well-being of beasts including cheetah and leopard. Richard Montali, opposite, views biopsies and blood smears from pathology lab through stereo-scopic microscope.

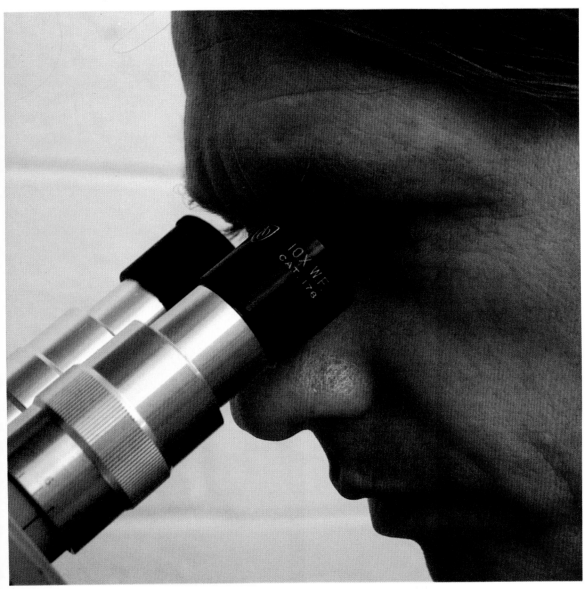

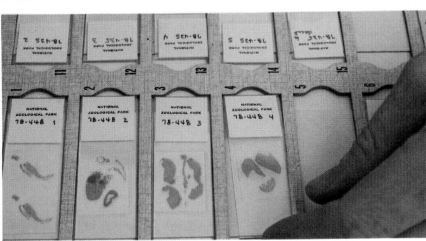

afflictions humans suffer, including TB, gout, parasites, fungal infections, and cancer.

During an average year more than 2,000 animals may receive medical care or be under close observation by the veterinary staff. Of these, more than 400 may be hospitalized, for an average stay of 28 days. The Zoo uses modern equipment including a Coulter counter to count blood cells, a refractometer to check total protein in the blood, and a computer to store the pathological data.

The end of the medical line at the National Zoo—if daily caretaking and preventive medicine and veterinary skill have all failed to stop an animal's death—is the performance of a necropsy, or autopsy. In a gleaming theater in the new Pathology Building, every death—be it that of a giraffe or a shrew—is investigated. The facility features a large walk-in refrigerator, adequate laboratory and storage space, and an overhead track for conveying deceased large animals, which then are deposited on a specially designed surgical table around which are gathered some of the best minds in the medical world. The necropsy team is determined to find, through studying the animals' organs, what the agent of death may have been. Many deaths hold a surprise, and every animal teaches us something to better help the living.

It's all very well to know that captive kangaroos often suffer from "lumpy jaw," a disease of teeth and supporting bone that leads to health breakdown. But how does this really happen? Leaning intensely over the table, these young doctors may succeed in solving that and other pertinent secrets of exotic animal life.   □

Performing autopsy on kangaroo at right, Dr. Montali and Dr. Jack Hoopes focus on death at the Zoo (down to 18 percent in 1978). Drama takes place in theater of Pathology Building, designed for maximum biohazard containment.

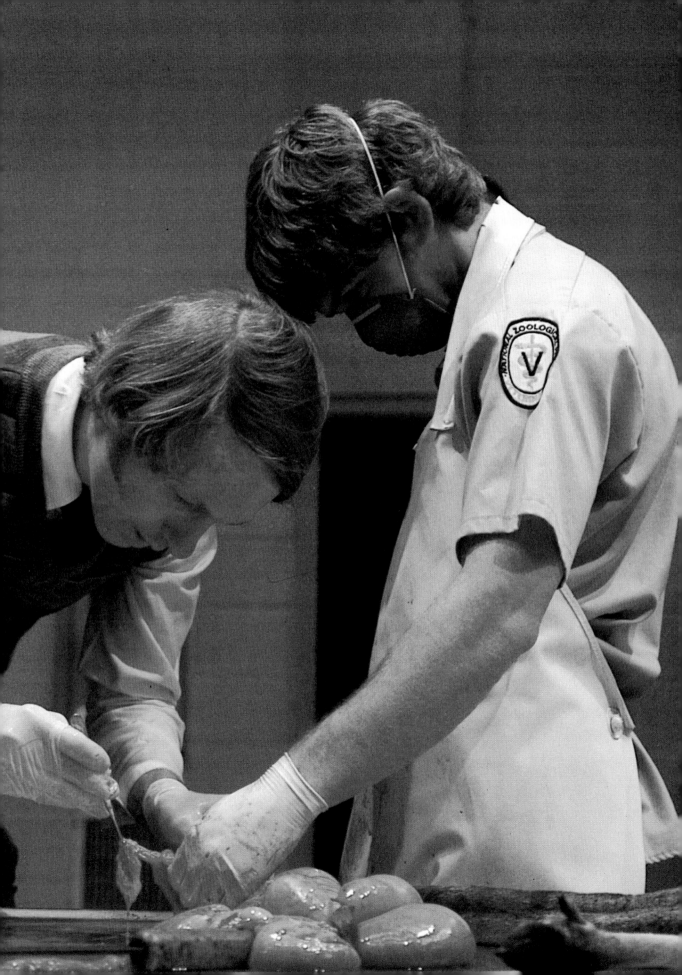

SECTION III
THE HEART OF THE MATTER

LOOKING CLOSELY

THE MYSTERIES OF BEHAVIOR

Janet L. Hopson

Zoologists travel tens of thousands of miles each year to study howler monkeys swinging through jungles, lions stalking their prey, and bejeweled butterflies sipping from orchids. Yet only a few dozen blocks from the U.S. Capitol, howlers swing, lions stalk, and butterflies sip nectar. Obviously, certain animal activities can be studied only under natural conditions. For other sorts of instinctive behavior, however, the Zoo offers a ready-made laboratory with exotic and interesting beasts just a short walk from the nearest bus line.

The interactions between mothers and babies offer one good example of instinctive behavior that remains virtually unchanged in many animals whether in the bush or in the cage. Difficult to study in the wild since denning and secrecy are often part of defending the young, maternal-infant behavior among captive animals is far easier to observe.

In the spring of 1977, Zoo researchers Katherine Ralls and Karl Kranz began a massive study of the mother-young relationships of hoofed animals in captivity. Volunteer observers spent more than 700 hours watching 20 individual babies of 10 ungulate species —oryx, wildebeest, bongo, sable, reindeer, pygmy hippo, Nile hippo, dorcas gazelle, giraffe, and waterbuck. The following year, the program was expanded to include mother and baby tapirs, Bactrian camels, zebras, Dorsett sheep, Père David's deer, muntjacs (small Indian deer), dik-diks (tiny African antelope), and markhor (goat-like animals from Pakistan). Most were housed at the National Zoo, a few observed at other facilities.

Some of these animals had been studied in the wild, but the reports of mother-young behavior were spotty. The National Zoo study aimed at observing similar features of *each*

Red panda cubs in their den, below. Top, keeper David Kessler holds cub by scruff, painlessly preventing it from resisting.

species, so that researchers could draw meaningful conclusions about ungulate maternal behavior in general.

The study focused on the well-known phenomena of "hiding" and "following" by baby ungulates. Some infants, the "followers," stay close to their mothers from the time they wobble to their feet until they get much older. Others, the "hiders," spend their early lives lying quietly amongst rocks or underbrush a distance away from where their mothers graze.

According to Dr. Ralls, a hider is isolated, inactive, and concealed for most of its early life, making it unlikely that a predator will see or hear it. Moreover, the mother usually eats the afterbirth, drinks the urine, and eats the feces of the baby during the hiding stage. It is thought that in some species the baby's scent glands do not produce scent for the first weeks of life. These factors thus make it difficult for a predator to find a baby by smell.

Indeed, hiding is so advantageous that the question arises as to why there are species in which babies do not hide. "To understand this," writes Ralls in a recent Zoo brochure, "one must know that most of the hiders belong to species in which the father plays no part in defending his offspring. Defense of the baby is up to the mother alone, and she may be helpless against predators much larger than she is or that travel in packs. Other species, like zebras, belong to a tightly knit family group containing a stallion who helps defend the baby. In a sense, these young are 'hiding' in a dense herd of their own species rather than in vegetation."

Although the Zoo mothers and babies live in fenced paddocks, the study still presented numerous challenges. Kranz, for example, acknowledging that "a lot of people think it's a piece of cake to do research in a zoo," occasionally spent more than an hour just locating a baby dik-dik before he could begin his regular observation period.

By the end of the second year, the Zoo researchers were able to place most of the species on a theoretical scale of proficiency at hiding and following. The pygmy hippo, for instance, is an excellent follower and, in fact, spends most of its early life actually touching its mother. Young wildebeests are proficient followers, reindeer a bit less so, and oryx babies spend still less time than the others in proximity to mothers and safety. Baby dik-diks, as Kranz found out the hard way, are excellent hiders. Sable, waterbuck, and dor-

Giraffe and offspring soon after birth. Born with relatively well-developed legs, young giraffes usually stand within an hour of birth.

cas gazelle young conceal themselves well, while bongo babies emerge from hiding much earlier than the others.

This study provided the Zoo's animal keepers with important management information on how long the young of each species must remain with their mothers before independently joining a new herd in a different paddock. The hider-follower continuum should also form a useful framework for future researchers, enabling them to understand the sometimes confusing behavior of young animals. Zoologists have had trouble in the past deciding whether various members of the sheep and goat family, for example, are followers or hiders. Perhaps the young of these ungulates may simply fall somewhere along the continuum between the two extremes.

Great interest in breeding captive animals underlies much of the in-house research effort at the National Zoo—and with good rea-

Devra Kleiman recording panda sounds, part of her research on panda reproduction.

son. Even relatively abundant species have become expensive and difficult to export from their native habitats. And as the rolls of endangered and threatened animals continue to grow, it is likely that, in the future, zoos will be required to prove their prowess at breeding captive animals before they can obtain rare specimens.

If zoos are to become net producers of wildlife rather than net consumers, their zoologists must create optimum reproductive conditions whose essential elements are frequently unknown for animals in the wild. It's twice the gamble, then, to transport those poorly understood animals or birds to a park in the midst of a large city and hope they will do what comes naturally. Zoologists must therefore collect considerable field data on mating, parental care, and feeding and social interactions in the wild, and then try to establish similar conditions in a zoo.

Even the best efforts sometimes fail, as in the case of Ling-Ling and Hsing-Hsing, the Zoo's giant pandas. Since April 1972, when two fuzzy black-and-white cubs arrived and enthralled the public with their antics, researchers' delight has shifted to concern over their sexual ineptitude. Despite several mating bouts in successive years, the pandas remained cubless through summer 1979.

Devra Kleiman, reproduction zoologist for the Zoo's Office of Zoological Research, had been worried for several years about the pandas' mating problems. The best available evidence suggested that pandas become reproductively senile at about 15 years of age. The American pandas were approaching the age of 8, and the remaining opportunities to produce cubs seemed dangerously few considering Hsing-Hsing's tendency to mount im-

properly and Ling-Ling's habit of falling over at just the wrong moment. Then, in June 1979, it was decided to obtain sperm from Hsing-Hsing for possible artificial insemination of the female the following spring. A comprehensive medical team under Zoo veterinarian Mitch Bush twice extracted sperm from Hsing-Hsing, who was anesthetized for each procedure and recovered with no visible ill effects.

Dr. Kleiman, however, still feels slightly uncomfortable with the notion of the "technological fix" in captive breeding. "With all of our expertise in artificial insemination of domestic animals like cattle, sheep, and pigs," she says, "we still can't apply all of the semen storage techniques successfully to an equally common animal—the horse." A species' estrous cycle must also be thoroughly understood before the technique is possible. "And we would be happy to have that data for as many as 15 percent of the species at the Zoo!" Thus semen storage, artificial insemination, and test-tube zoo animals remain, for the most part, a thing of the future.

Kleiman prefers a behavioral approach to understanding an animal's mating cycle and has, accordingly, instituted careful observation periods and check sheets. Assisted by volunteers and students, Kleiman keeps a detailed record of the pandas' appetites, activity levels, and other tell-tale signs of sexual readiness ("bleating," pacing, scent marking, and ano-genital rubbing). Panda night watches and morning watches take place in November, March (just before mating season), and April (when Ling-Ling usually begins her heat period). By charting the combined results of these watches, Kleiman and the keepers can determine the most propitious time each year to place the pandas together. In addition, the giant pandas' mating difficulties suggested to Kleiman that the animals might be overweight. Ling-Ling, in particular, seemed unable to support the combined heavy weight of the pair during mounting. She was subsequently placed on a diet (fewer bamboo shoots and less rice) with results that remain to be seen.

Night watches (and sometimes round-the-clock watches) have been used for other problem breeders as well, such as red pandas and rhinos. Trends emerging from these observations have enabled the Zoo staff to improve space requirements, food and social groupings, and, in turn, the production and survival of babies.

One summer, for example, a mother red (or

lesser) panda began to carry her infants nervously about the enclosure, at times dangling them dangerously as she climbed up and down trees. It was finally determined that the mother red panda was displaying an instinctive "infant-hiding response" and needed a simple adjustment—a second nest box in her enclosure—to put her at ease. She could then transfer the litter back and forth between the boxes. Accordingly, the stress level—and altitude—dropped for both mother and young.

Detailed information from cheetah watches revealed that the continual presence of adult males agitated and reproductively suppressed the adult females. Separating them looked imperative if the females were ever to come into heat. This and similar adjustments have increased the number of cheetahs born in captivity 40- or 50-fold in recent years.

In 1972, rhino watchers were able to document the events before, during, and after the spectacular mating bout of two Indian rhinoceroses. The rhinos were allowed access to each other on and off for several months before the female's estrus, and this proximity increased their desires to the boiling point by late summer. Playful horn nuzzling, mud wallowing, charging, urine squirting, whistling, and prancing were observed in the weeks just before mating. And 15 months after the climactic, day-long sexual marathon, a calf was born.

An adult Bactrian camel chasing and nipping a juvenile, top. Above, Patrick with his mother. He was the first Indian rhino born in North America.

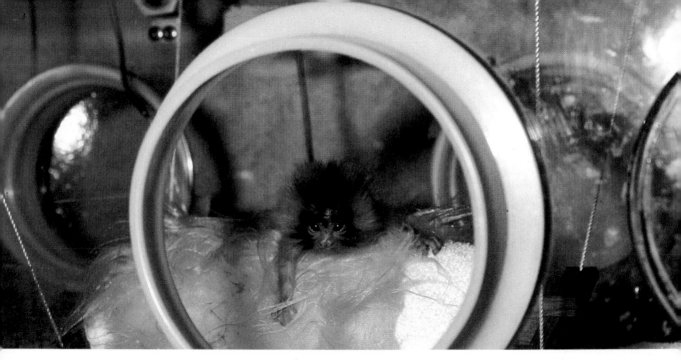

Infant golden lion marmoset clutches fluff-covered surrogate mother in incubator. Abused by her mother, she was hand reared, then successfully reintroduced to marmoset family.

Successful breeders, however, can sometimes turn into problem breeders. Attempts to interest the rhinos in a second mating have failed dismally. It is not clear whether the female has even experienced hormonal cycling since the birth. Researchers thus began taking urine samples for hormone analysis. By analyzing urine and comparing the hormone levels from a regularly and irregularly cycling rhino female, the Zoo hopes to detect estrus more accurately and, in turn, encourage more successful breeding.

If a majority of zoo animals were problem breeders, the position of reproduction zoologist would be both frustrating and dull. Luckily, however, some zoo animals reproduce prolifically. And the research has its special rewards when a conducive mating climate is so well established that an animal literally doomed to extinction can be brought back in great numbers.

The golden lion marmoset, a South American monkey thought by some to be the most beautiful mammal on the planet, is such an animal. The adults are tiny (1 to 2 pounds) and are covered with shiny gold hair. Most prominent of all are their metallic golden manes, arching backward from their alert faces to cloak their small shoulders. Intelligent and active, the animals have unfortunately suffered one massive quirk of fate: they evolved and adapted over millions of years to the small forested region near what was to become Rio de Janeiro, one of South America's largest cities.

In 1500, virtually the entire area was covered with dense forest. By 1975, fully 98 percent of the land had been harvested for tropical hardwoods, cleared for agriculture, or covered with towns, cities, and roads. Besides the near-total destruction of their habitat, golden marmosets have always been prized as pets, are relatively easy to catch, and are the closest primate species to Brazil's major port. "You put all those factors together," Kleiman observes, "and you have an extinct animal."

The best current estimates suggest that no more than 250 golden lion marmosets survive in the wild. Furthermore, until 1972, zoo populations were breeding so poorly that it seemed certain the "most beautiful mammal" would be extinct within a decade.

That same year, however, the National Zoo hosted an international conference on the biology of these and related monkey species. And, in a sense, the energy and inspiration generated at that meeting changed the fate of the golden lion marmoset.

Kleiman and the National Zoo made a special commitment then to study the animal's reproductive problems in captivity. With the help of students, volunteers, and animal keepers, Kleiman kept careful daily observations of the marmoset's eating habits and reproductive and social behavior.

So little was known of their food preferences in the wild that the zoo menus turned out to be thoroughly inappropriate. Marmosets had long been fed a basic diet of fruit, but they needed considerable amounts of protein as well. When cottage cheese, eggs, and small, hairless mouse pups were added to their diet, the monkeys' reproductive success and life-span increased dramatically.

Marmosets, physically delicate creatures, succumb easily to intestinal parasites, colds, and viruses. The tiny amount of measles virus transmitted from a healthy boy or girl visitor with a recent measles vaccination could infect and wipe out a marmoset colony in less than a week. For this reason, the Zoo now keeps its golden marmosets strictly isolated from visitors and other Zoo animals. One large colony maintained at the Tijuca Bank of Lion Marmosets in Rio de Janeiro suffered a disastrous loss recently, when more than 30 animals died of an unidentified disease. Isolation and daily observation of the rare monkeys make a similar loss much less likely at the National Zoo.

But perhaps the biggest success in Kleiman's study of golden lion marmoset breeding involved the discovery of what could be called the "teenage baby-sitting syndrome." Marmosets live in family groups consisting of a pair of adults and offspring of varying ages. Older juveniles can start to breed after about 18 months but are repressed from doing so if left with their parents. For many years, therefore, it was standard policy to remove the juveniles and pair them with unrelated mates as early as possible. A simian Catch-22, however, flawed this approach: these early-separated young adults bred prolifically—but they made miserable parents, ignoring, mutilating, or killing their babies.

Kleiman, student Robert Hoage, and other workers found that the juveniles must be left with the parents until a second group of young are born and raised. By baby-sitting the new youngsters from time to time, the "teens" learn how to be good parents.

In 1972 only 69 golden lion marmosets existed in captivity. Now there are well over 100. Most of that increase has been in the National Zoo's colony, which has grown from two breeding pairs to more than 50 animals.

People often speak of reintroducing captive-bred animals to the wild. Will some of these Zoo-born golden marmosets ever be replanted in the forests near Rio to renew the small natural population? "The chances of that are slim," says Kleiman, "at least for the foreseeable future. There is no real suitable habitat left, and the captive-born animals would have to be taught to fend for themselves in the wild." This teaching process would involve hiring researchers, building a "halfway house," controlling predators, reforesting the area, constructing nest boxes, supplemental feeding, and, above all, finding a large and continual flow of cash for the project. In short, an unlikely prospect.

For now, marmoset-lovers must be content with a viable population in captivity and with the promise that this isolated bit of genetic diversity, their beautiful and exotic monkey, will be around for the education of another human generation. And perhaps people may ultimately be inspired to return the marmoset's habitat to its former condition.

* * *

Zoological research itself can be placed on a continuum from very practical to extremely theoretical. For an institution dedicated to

A mother marmoset with offspring. Monogamous, adults share rearing chores, as do adolescents.

breeding and rearing rare animals, panda pampering and baby watching are practical projects, indeed. But theories can be just as interesting and important in the long run. Zoo researcher Eugene S. Morton recently devised an idea with enormous evolutionary significance—nothing less than the Rosetta stone of animal communication.

Animals make a wide range of vocal sounds—squeals, chirps, bleats, rumbles, growls, twitters, clicks. But what do they *mean*? For years, says Dr. Morton, people have examined individual sounds from a single species and wondered what *specific* meaning has, say, the grunt of a guinea pig or the whine of a sparrow hawk. Does the grunt mean "I want my pellets" or "You're standing in my way"? Does the whine mean "Let's lay beautiful eggs together" or "Let's raid a chicken coop"?

Morton wondered about animal sounds, too, but took an entirely different approach. He looked for the elements that animal language has in common, then asked *why* those elements are shared. His approach paid off.

The key to universal animal language, he postulates, is simple, consisting of the growl, the bark, and the whine. Throughout the animal world, says Morton, from bobwhites and barn swallows to elephants and wombats, an angry animal growls, a frightened, submissive, or friendly animal whines, and an aroused animal barks.

Granted, that sounds odd. Birds barking and growling? Elephants whining? If, however, you discount the human onomatopoetic renditions of animals' sounds (i.e., that owls *rasp*, purple martins *sweeet*, and rhesus monkeys *roar*, etc.) and look, instead, for the acoustical common denominators in animal sounds, the three basics are indeed the low, harsh growl; the high, tonal whine; and the abrupt bark with sound rising, then falling.

These three sounds sufficiently define the entire vocal repertoire, and the innumerable sounds falling in between can all be described in relation to them. A screech can thus be seen as an aggressive growl combined with a high, tonal whine of fear that, together, say, "I am terribly frightened, but will stand and fight if pushed any further."

Morton is an ornithologist by training, and it's really no surprise that an ornithologist cracked this animal code. Students of the bird world commonly employ a large instrument called a sonograph in their work to create two-dimensional pictures of bird songs. It takes years to learn to read a sonogram correctly so that the scratchy lines actually translate into mental sounds, just as notes on a staff become an internalized melody to a musician reading sheet music.

After staring at thousands of these sonograms of bird and animal sounds, the theory coalesced for Morton. He realized that the two-dimensional *shapes* of the omnipresent growls, whines, and barks were the same on paper regardless of whether, to us, the animal's voice is low, slow, and deafening, or high, fast, and flute-like. On the sonograms, growls appear as thick, low-frequency bands. Whines are high, thin lines. And chirps or barks are chevron shapes with up and down lines. *Voilà!* The Rosetta stone.

Once Morton realized this, he had a handle for grasping an even more important concept—*why* this system is the same for creatures as different as birds and elephants. Why couldn't birds whine when they are angry and growl when afraid, and elephants do the reverse? Or vice versa?

The reason, Morton says, is that evolution selected this particular system because it saves everybody considerable time and energy. The earliest land animals, he explains, probably had no voices at all. Primitive amphibians such as salamanders still don't. When an animal with no voice wants to keep a particular patch of foraging land for itself, it must literally fight off every intruder. This goes as well for claiming mates and perches and burrows.

This fighting system would promote the survival of larger and larger animals, since a big creature can usually win a fight with a smaller one. And the gigantism once common in reptiles, birds, and mammals was no doubt due in part to this selection for great size. But largeness has at least one big disadvantage—the animal has an enormous appetite. And so does fighting constantly— no time to satiate that huge appetite. Accordingly, nature evolved a better system— the variable voice.

Physically, the vocal cords of a large animal can make a lower, harsher sound than the voice apparatus of a small animal. Therefore, if a small animal makes a low, harsh sound, it *seems bigger*. And that fact alone may scare off an intruder on its turf or a competitor for its mate. Then, rather than fighting, both animals can go back to eating, mating, or related activities. The growl substitutes for combat itself.

Conversely, a smaller animal such as an infant makes a higher tonal sound. Therefore, if an animal—even a big one—wants to show appeasement, friendliness, or fear, it can simply whine. This will mollify its competitor, parent, or mate, and it can avoid the trouble of running off to hide or being thrashed, starved, or ignored. The bark, last of all, shows that something of interest is perceived which is neither frightening nor aggression-inducing. With this sound, a bird in a flock, let's say, can keep its friends attentive, lending protection and support.

"To put this theory in a few words," says Morton, "the *sounds* of largeness have replaced the need to *be* large, and the sounds of *smallness* the need to *be* small. It's really a beautiful system."

It applies, as well, to the emotional components of human language. Adult "baby talk" is higher and softer than the normal speaking voice—an instinctive way to appease, reduce fear, or show love. Threatening phrases ("I'll murder you!") are usually delivered with a lower, harsher tone. And interest words like "Hey!" and "Wow!" are usually emotionally neutral, or balanced.

The marks of an elegant scientific theory are simplicity and applicability, and Mor-

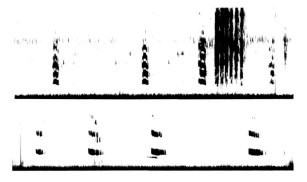

A Carolina wren, top. It is one of the species whose sounds have been analyzed by Eugene Morton in a study of animal communication. Above, two wren sonograms, representing "low barks," upper, and "fright sounds," lower.

Young dik-diks are "hiders," spending much of early life lying concealed some distance away from grazing mothers. Other species, "followers," stay close to mothers.

ton's hypothesis on universal animal language is strong on both. It may not be immediately applicable to zoo management (although someday keepers may even learn to speak rudimentary Camel or Hippo). But it does have enormous potential for clarifying the meaning and evolution of animal sounds. And that's quite a bit for a single idea.

* * *

Blue whales are the largest animals that ever lived on earth, reaching 100 feet in length and weighing as much as 24 elephants. A blue whale heart alone can weigh 1,300 pounds. Since female blue whales are bigger than males, the largest animal with the greatest heart that ever beat was surely a female blue whale.

The moral here is neither ecological nor social, but biological. It is seldom recognized that, among many mammal species, the females are larger than their mates. And this affects their survival, their ability to raise young, and their tendency to choose one mate rather than several. None of this was recognized at all, in fact, until National Zoo researcher Katherine Ralls turned her attention to the subject of big females.

Among insects, fish, and reptiles, large females are quite common. But by surveying the size data on mammals, Dr. Ralls found a surprisingly long list of species—more than 100—in which the females are larger than the males. When one takes a large stack of seemingly disparate information and sifts from it a smaller pile of related facts, one is in a position to form new and important generalizations. And Ralls did precisely that.

Beginning with Charles Darwin, she says, biologists have emphasized the role of largeness in winning mates. Since males often compete with each other for mates, and are also usually larger, the former is assumed to have dictated the latter. But, says Ralls, mate competition and largeness don't go hand in hand among females. They neither fight for males, nor have the teeth, antlers, and other features needed for combat. Their size, instead, is the result of the evolutionary pressure to be proficient mothers.

A big mother can produce larger, healthier, and more numerous young than can a small mother. A large mother can also yield larger quantities of milk and more easily fend off predators. As long as there is enough around for *her* to eat, the larger mother is in a better position to survive and pass along her genes in the form of offspring.

Biologists, says Ralls, should stop looking at a mammal's size from a male perspective—i.e., that the female is the "standard" size for the species and that the male has grown larger or smaller during the course of evolution due to sexual competition. Size should be seen, she says, from a two-sex perspective; male size due to certain evolutionary pressures, and female size due to others.

This entire question of size fits neatly into a second concept—that of monogamy among mammals. Devra Kleiman has looked closely at this single-mate approach to breeding and has created a tidy synthesis from apparently disparate data.

Dr. Kleiman finds two general "life styles" for single-mate mammals, with various intermediates falling in between. One extreme is best characterized by the elephant shrews, rat-like African animals with elongated, flexible snouts. The males and females live separately and mate solely with each other out of necessity, not love—there are usually too few partners to go around. They rarely interact with each other at all, and the female alone raises the young. The male's contribution is indirect; he defends the resources of their joint territory against intruders. The young elephant shrews are booted out and find their own home range some distance away from the aggressive parents.

The other type of monogamy is best exemplified by the golden lion marmoset of Brazil. The male and female bond strongly and exclusively out of preference for each other and rarely "cheat." They work equally to raise the young and keep the teenagers around to help bring up the next offspring.

Although quite different, both mating systems are successful strategies for survival and reproduction. They do share, however, two interesting traits. First, monogamous males and females tend to look and act quite alike, and often the female is larger than the male. Second, intense sexual activity at the beginning of the relationship trails off into a comfortable "marriage" of companionship—in other words, the honeymoon ends.

Both of these shared traits hold fascination for Kleiman and Ralls. Body size, particularly the occurrence of large females, may be a handy clue to monogamous pair-bonding in those many species whose mating habits are still unknown. And the short-honeymoon syndrome has widespread implications for understanding animal behavior—including our own.

This combined understanding of monogamy and body size has already improved the husbandry of certain zoo animals. In many antelope species, for instance, the males are much larger and more aggressive than the females and have "harems." The diminutive dik-dik, however, has slightly larger females. Captive dik-diks had routinely been kept in herds—a fact which ultimately militated against their breeding success. Kleiman and colleagues suspected, from their body size and other habits, that dik-diks should be kept in monogamous pairs, not herds. Since they split up the herds, the National Zoo has developed the nation's most successful program for breeding dik-diks in captivity.

The scientists and students at the Office of Zoological Research have gained prominence for their careful, creative approach and for their practical and theoretical studies.

Devra Kleiman sums it up this way: "I think we have a unique group of people whose research talents work together. We overlap but don't compete, and the result is progress in applied zoo work, theoretical research, ecology, and conservation. It all goes around and around," she says, "and it's just kind of beautiful to watch." □

A young muntjac, also a hider, stands rigidly still in the underbrush.

PANDA WATCH

Ever since their arrival from China in 1972, the giant pandas Ling-Ling and Hsing-Hsing have been the Zoo's most popular attraction. But, their status as celebrities notwithstanding, the pandas have yet to produce the offspring Zoo officials have hoped for. As one wag wrote in a Washington newspaper not long ago, "Ling-Ling and Hsing-Hsing still haven't done a thing-thing."

Unfortunately, little is known about the reproductive behavior of pandas in captivity. Even less is known about it in the wild. As a result, Zoo researchers are now compiling base-line data by closely observing the pair.

Because pandas in the wild are solitary, and because in captivity they occasionally fight, Ling-Ling and Hsing-Hsing are kept in separate enclosures and paddocks, though wire-mesh windows allow them ample visual and olfactory contact with each other. When Ling-Ling comes into heat, however, the barrier between them is removed.

The lack of breeding success thus far may result from several factors. But there is one encouraging note. Ling-Ling and Hsing-Hsing appear to be compatible. Chinese zoo sources indicate that, in some instances, intended pairs proved so flagrantly incompatible that sexual interest by one or the other was rebuffed in the clearest of terms. Fortunately, Ling-Ling and Hsing-Hsing enjoy climbing "furniture" and exploring new obstacles together. Perhaps that, in time, will lead to more. □

Ling-Ling and Hsing-Hsing, far lower left, eye each other through mesh window. At left, they munch on bamboo, in this case having chosen to dine together. With Ling-Ling in heat, above, the two engage in sexual preliminaries, which include rough-and-tumble play as well as scent marking, seen in upper right. At lower right, Hsing-Hsing attempts to copulate.

TENRECS AND QUILLS

OUT IN THE FIELD

Janet L. Hopson

Nearly halfway around the world from the meandering paths and green enclosures of the National Zoo, the lush, tropical island of Madagascar rises out of the Indian Ocean. A great deal of research takes place in the same distant places where zoo specimens themselves are found, and Madagascar is an active location for members of the National Zoo's Office of Zoological Research.

The fourth largest island in the world, this verdant land remains remote in both space and time. The eastern coast of Africa—the nearest continent—lies 250 miles away across the Mozambique Channel. And the many strange plants and animals that still populate Madagascar's rain forests and central plateau bear testimony to the island's long, slow evolution in utter isolation.

Giant browsing primates, elephant birds twice as tall as a man, and enormous land tortoises once roamed the island. While they are now gone, in their place remain creatures nearly as primitive: the civet, mongoose, and ring-tailed lemur, for example. And, in addition, the striped tenrec.

A number of years ago, John Eisenberg, now Assistant Director of the Zoo, became fascinated with the fauna of Madagascar and chose to study that obscure group of insect-eating mammals called tenrecs. These odd creatures lack the drama of their giant ancestors and the complexity of their living island cousins, but could yet prove the most strangely interesting mammals of all.

Dr. Eisenberg describes the tenrecs as the

A striped tenrec's dorsal quills, magnified here several times, produce ultrasonic sound.

Domestic elephants owned by the Smithsonian carry researchers and paraphernalia for the

Smithsonian-Nepalese tiger survey across a plain in Nepal's Royal Chitawan National Park.

nearest to the *Urtier*, the fundament, the prototype creatures from which all mammals evolved (save the marsupials of Australia). More than 100 million years ago, Madagascar was wrenched loose from Africa and drifted slowly eastward, carrying along its reptiles, birds, and the small shrew-like creatures that would later radiate into the grand and varied class Mammalia on both land masses. But the pressures to change were slower and less intense on the isolated protomammals of Madagascar than on their African counterparts. The tenrecs of today are thus closer to these ancient prototypes than any other living animal. "We all," says Eisenberg, "hark back to a generalized tenrec."

Eisenberg and colleague Edwin Gould observed and described this group of primitive mammals more extensively than any naturalists had before them. In the process, they discovered a remarkable form of communication in one group member, the striped tenrec. This animal when fully grown is only 6 inches long. It wears a skunk-like warning flag of black and yellow stripes—and a cov-

ering of spines and hollow quills to enforce the threat implicit in its coloration. With its pointed snout and its forward-thrusting crown of spines, it resembles a Walt Disney character, both malevolent and slightly silly. Despite its humorous appearance, however, the striped tenrec is a well-adapted, self-protected machine, consuming its own body weight in earthworms each day. The animals forage continually in the damp leaf litter of the forest floor, only occasionally falling prey to a boa constrictor or mongoose.

Eisenberg and Dr. Gould noticed a suspicious-looking patch of vibrating quills on each adult's back, and discovered that they actually produce a high-frequency sound called "stridulation." This odd form of sound occurs above the range of human hearing and is detectable to us only by means of special electronic equipment. Animals stridulate when feeding, courting, exploring, or fleeing predators. But it most commonly occurs among mothers with young.

By observing several families from the vantage point of a bamboo-and-wood scaf-

A herd of wild Asiatic elephants gathers into a protective cluster as an old cow stations herself in front of the group. Researchers discovered the importance of the elephant matriarchy.

folding high above a large fenced area, Eisenberg and Gould found that a mother tenrec creates a steady hum with her quill patch while foraging. This "white noise" in turn helps the young stay in safe proximity while learning how and where to harvest worms for themselves. If she stops her "quill talk," they scurry in the direction she was last heard.

This odd mechanism, says Eisenberg, is precisely analogous to the clucking of a mother hen—a steady background signal that says, "All is well, keep foraging." Because a mother tenrec has her pointed snout in the dirt most of the time, rooting out worms, her quills make the signal for her.

The tenrecs, even those without protective quills or special communication systems, have all the standard equipment one associates with mammals, including the five senses and distinct patterns of maternal and social behavior. Carnivores, elephants, and even humans may have larger brains and more sophisticated learning capacities. "But these abilities are all just accretions on the basic plan of how to organize time and energy," explains Eisenberg. "We are not much different from tenrecs in the long run."

Any comparison between the small, primitive tenrec and the stately elephant may seem tenuous indeed. But a separate study of these great beasts by John Eisenberg revealed some remarkable similarities and, more important, some critical information needed in the fight to save the creatures from extinction.

Like the tenrec project, the Smithsonian elephant study took place on another tropical island in the Indian Ocean, Sri Lanka. The modern and conservation-minded government of that ancient agricultural land had asked the Smithsonian for help in assessing and preserving their shrinking population of Asiatic elephants. Eisenberg and three colleagues, Melvyn Lockhart, George McKay, and Fred Kurt, launched a long-term study of the elephants (and other mammals) in three Sri Lankan national parks.

The behavior and ecology of wild Asiatic elephants had never before really been examined. This is curious, considering their utter visibility and their long association with humankind as beasts of burden, as sources of meat and precious ivory, and as instruments of war. But, explains Eisenberg, elephants are actually quite hard to find without an expert tracker. They are shy of observers and they can be dangerous if approached. On top of that, once safely located, watching the adults can be exceedingly boring.

An elephant's stupendous proportions help clarify that last point. An adult Asiatic elephant stands 9 to 10 feet high and can weigh up to 11,000 pounds. To sustain itself in the wild, an adult must each day eat over 200 pounds of grass and other forage, and drink 15 gallons of water. Hence adult elephants spend about *19 hours* per day sorting and chewing their food—a pastime that, for the human observer, grows monumentally dull in no time.

In the remaining time each day, these rugged creatures spend just two or three hours sleeping and devote the rest to bathing and caring for their thick but sensitive hide. The antics of bathing juveniles, romping and hosing each other with water, provided the full-time Smithsonian viewers with comic relief. But their observations of elephant-style child care revealed the previously unknown basis of elephant society: the matriarchy.

Females form the cohesive unit in the elephant world, living together in herds, caring for the young, and staking out large home ranges that merely overlap those of the solitary bulls. Since adult females must eat almost continually, baby-sitting becomes a problem. Thus each day, one cow—somewhat reluctantly—takes charge of the kindergarten and keeps an eye (and a nose) out for predators.

It is the elephant's pattern of maternal behavior, according to Eisenberg, that so strikingly resembles the behavior of small and simple tenrecs. If, for example, a stranger is introduced to a colony of tenrecs, they will crowd around him, just as do elephants with a newcomer. If a mother tenrec is agitated by a strange creature or object, she will often approach it while the young stay back. Similarly, younger female elephants and infants remain behind while an older, dominant female approaches a curious new disturbance. Perhaps most striking is that both female elephants and female tenrecs (of certain species) lead their young from place to place in long, single-file parades, rather than in close huddles.

These similarities underscore the basic "mammalian plan" represented by the tenrecs, and show that when one looks closely enough, many essential solutions to survival problems are the same despite enormous physical differences between species.

The Smithsonian Asiatic elephant study on Sri Lanka had considerable practical importance, as well as general implications for un-

A male Asiatic elephant takes time out from its browsing to bathe.

derstanding the animal kingdom. The Smithsonian team presented that nation's wildlife authorities a series of recommendations for protecting the remaining wild elephants. Those centered on the creation of buffer zones between agricultural fields and park land to discourage crop damage by elephants, and the expansion of park boundaries so that sufficient habitat would remain to support large, viable elephant herds.

The team's study methods and basic findings also laid the groundwork for elephant research in Malaysia. The data from these studies are being combined now to create a conservation plan for all the elephant populations remaining in India and Southeast Asia, an undertaking of immense importance if future generations are to enjoy these mammoth creatures in their natural habitat or in zoological parks.

* * *

Polonnaruwa, an ancient Sri Lankan ruin now overrun by jungle, was the site of two additional studies—these on monkeys—by National Zoo researchers.

During the 11th century A.D., the high middle ages of Sri Lankan history, Polonnaruwa was a royal city, the capital of a powerful Buddhist kingdom. Over the centuries, the kings had created an intricate system of dams and lakes to irrigate rice paddies and, by so doing, enabled a large human population to prosper in the area. This did not, however, prevent their ultimate destruction by war. And the ruins, now overgrown by tropical rain forest and resembling a Rudyard Kipling scene, have been inherited largely by monkey troops.

Zoologists Rasanayagam Rudran and Wolfgang P. J. Dittus studied, respectively,

121

Howler monkeys perch on a branch, below. Recent research on howlers documents infanticide by aggressive outside males. Bottom, an infant red howler monkey, a victim of such an attack, lies in the litter of the forest floor.

the purple-faced langurs and the toque macaques now living at Polonnaruwa and nearby sites. Unlike many recent studies, however, the two researchers were concerned with the primates not as models for understanding human behavior, but as unique social organisms. Through this fresh zoological perspective, they were able to witness behavior patterns such as infanticide, and to understand the strange, lopsided death statistics for young monkeys.

Dr. Rudran was intrigued by male "takeovers" among the purple-faced langurs. These brown monkeys, with their reddish-purple faces and bristling white beards, live almost exclusively in small troops of females and young, headed by a single male. Every now and then a new, aggressive male will appear, fight, and chase off the troop's previous male and assume leadership.

During or soon after the coup, the infants and juveniles also disappear from the troop. Their absence causes the adult females to begin estrus—and the new male avails himself of the opportunity. But what became of the young? Why were they expelled? And how do these tumultuous takeovers benefit the troop in the long run?

Rudran deduced that the takeovers are,

Gray langurs suffer occasional infanticide when a new male takes over a breeding troop.

although seemingly violent and disruptive, biologically important. They assure "new blood" so the colony does not become inbred, and by dispersing the young they prevent overpopulation in one locale. These explanations, however, still left the mystery of the missing monkeys.

In science, puzzle pieces that eventually complete a larger pattern often come from distant places and even separate species. And in this case, Rudran found an answer to the question of the disappearing young in a Venezuelan forest.

Rudran was an eyewitness—for the first known time in South America—to infanticide by male red howler monkeys. During one troop takeover, a vicious bite from the alien male nearly severed an infant's tail, a wound which later proved fatal. A second infant was cruelly bitten in the head and died of massive skull fractures and blood loss.

It is likely that, back in Sri Lanka, infant purple-faced langurs meet the same fate when the troop leadership changes. Older juveniles may be able to flee the new male and try to survive on their own or join other troops. Infanticide by strange males has been explained as an attempt by the male to destroy a rival's offspring and then replace them with his own genetic stock. But Rudran thinks there may be a more immediate reason for infanticide: food. The young compete with the leader for limited food resources, and would also compete with his offspring once the latter were born into the troop. By killing or running off the existing young, the new leader assures himself and his progeny sufficient food.

The importance of food to primate social behavior was also noticed by Dr. Dittus in his study of the toque macaques that dwell in the trees around the Polonnaruwa ruins. He wondered why there seem to be so few female juveniles compared to male juveniles, and why the contrary—more females than males—is true among young adults.

Dawn-to-dusk observation of the olive-colored macaques revealed that the troop's social "pecking order" actually determines who is at the head of the bread line. The dominant male leaders eat well because they command access to the best feeding spots. The adult females get second best; the juvenile males third-rate cuisine; and the juvenile females the paltry leftovers. If these young females make it past their difficult youth, however, they have a good chance of survival to old age, for they are important to the colony as breeders and parents. Young adult males, on the other hand, have just begun their struggles, as they battle each other, sometimes fatally, over troop leadership.

This system may sound harsh, but in the end, says Dittus, it keeps the lid on population. When food is short, fewer young females survive to breeding age and the colony grows at a slower pace. The whole group, therefore, never completely devastates the existing food resources, which would lead to slow starvation for all. The population steam valve—the expendable young—would "blow" long before the food was gone, leaving the adults alive to start a new generation.

Food, of course, is not a limiting factor in zoos. Langurs and macaques in captivity eat like gourmets in the south of France, and can increase their numbers without fear of hunger or predation. But these behavioral field studies on primates have nonetheless helped researchers at the Zoo control and establish successful breeding colonies.

They now know, for instance, not to introduce a new male to a colony where there are infants younger than 10 months old. Even with abundant food, the old instincts can emerge, and a captive-born infant may be needlessly killed. The field studies also suggest that males may not develop an instinct for paternal care until after some critical age. Even if not an actual infant-killer, a young male may well make a poor father and should be bred at an older age than a female.

* * *

In August of 1974, a young but fierce male tiger emerged from a mangrove marsh in the Ganges River delta near Calcutta, India, and

approached the village of Jharkhali. Within a few hours a woman lay dead. The tiger also killed several domestic animals before it could be darted, immobilized, and caged.

In the past, man-killing tigers were invariably destroyed. But current Indian wildlife protection laws dictate that the animal must be saved unless incorrigibly homicidal. John Seidensticker, a large-cat expert and field researcher for the National Zoo, was flown in from Nepal. It was quickly decided to tranquilize the young animal, then transfer him to the nearby Sundarbans Tiger Reserve.

The slumbering tiger was placed in a zoo transfer cage and carried by boat to a release site in the delta reserve. Once awakened from the immobilization chemicals, the tiger walked off through the deep mud and into a thick stand of mangroves.

Four days later, Dr. Seidensticker and the Indian research team returned to the tiger reserve only to find the newly released tiger dead in his tracks, 25 feet from the cage—the victim of multiple, gaping wounds inflicted by a larger tiger.

This incident points out one immutable fact of wildlife management: working with large predators, particularly attempting to transplant them into new surroundings, is complicated, risky, and often unsuccessful. Some wild-born hoofed animals can be transferred from one range to another with

Game preserves and knowledge of tiger ecology may offer the only hope for these highly endangered big cats. Top, three men prepare to put a collar with a small radio transmitter on an immobilized Bengal tiger as part of an ongoing study of this subspecies in Nepal. A game reserve in Sariska, India, offers critical refuge to another tiger, above and opposite.

relative ease. Many game birds are now routinely hatched in captivity and reintroduced to the wild. But, as the Sundarbans tiger case proves, it's a different ball game altogether for large predators.

John Eisenberg is among the wildlife experts who are pessimistic about the prospects of reintroducing captive-born predators to the wild. "Born Free" operations in which a single large cat is hand reared and trained to hunt are extremely expensive. Reintroducing perhaps 10 tigers into the wild could take more than five years and cost more than one-half million dollars. And even at that, the tigers—having lost their natural fear and avoidance of humans—would always be particularly dangerous.

Dr. Eisenberg considers the translocation of wild-born predators a more viable option, but it too has drawbacks. The Sundarbans tiger was unwittingly placed in another tiger's home territory. And unless one of the two (probably the young intruder) had quickly migrated to another unclaimed territory, a death was inevitable. Clearly, researchers must learn considerably more about the home ranges and interactions of large predators before they can hope to successfully transplant them within wild habitats.

This is one of the reasons that the Smithsonian Institution has funded several studies of Asian cats. Seidensticker has observed the interactions of tigers and leopards in Nepal and studied the natural history of the Javan tiger (now virtually extinct, with just five individuals remaining). The work on tigers was continued by Melvin Sunquist and Kirti Tamang, and the Nepal study continues under the direction of zoologist David Smith, who is employing radio transmitters to help track tiger movements through the park.

Once detailed information has been collected regarding home ranges, movements, and prey, larger questions may be answered.

Is the Chitawan area large enough, and the terrain suitable, to ensure the survival of a genetically diverse and healthy population of tigers? If not, what should be done? And if it is sufficiently large, can isolated and doomed pockets of five and six tigers be safely translocated into the preserve?

It seems sometimes that the efforts to save magnificent wildlife like the Bengal tiger move forward too slowly. But as the Sundarbans tiger case demonstrated, without sufficient data on their habits and territories, precipitous actions to preserve large predators can instead end in their destruction.

* * *

One usually associates the zoological garden with ferocious animals, tropical birds, and exotic places. Many of the displays in North American zoos, however, are quite appropriately filled with North American animals. And, not surprisingly, those indigenous organisms have their own survival problems and unsolved mysteries. Thus National Zoo field researchers (particularly students and beginning workers) aim part of their efforts at organisms close to home.

Eugene Morton and his student Gee Gee Snyder recently developed a successful program to help the Eastern bluebird. This lovely and popular symbol of happiness is no longer a common American songbird. In just 40 years, its numbers have dropped by 90 percent. This drastic decline is due to loss of habitat, the impact of pesticides on its favorite insect species, and competition from that familiar imported duo, the English house sparrow and the starling.

Even when bluebirds are lucky enough to find a small cavity in a dead tree or a decaying fence post in which to lay their clutch of small eggs, a new generation is far from assured. Sparrows and starlings, if they find the nest, will puncture or toss out the eggs, peck the nestlings to death (sometimes also killing the adults), then build a new nest right over the carcasses. And even if the bluebirds can defend their nest from aggressive birds, their eggs and young are still at the mercy of bears, snakes, and raccoons searching for a meal.

To help save the vanishing bluebird, amateur ornithologists have constructed trails of bluebird houses, 100 yards apart, in open rural country with scattered trees and sparse ground cover. One such trail in western Canada (designed for a similar species, the Western bluebird) now stretches 2,000 miles and houses thousands of bluebirds each year.

Dr. Morton and Snyder built a trail of 36 bluebird nesting boxes at the National Zoo's Conservation and Research Center at Front Royal, Virginia, during the summer of 1975. They hoped to improve the rate of survival and, at the same time, study the bluebird's breeding and behavior. That first year, however, predation by natural enemies was extremely high, and less than one-third of the young survived to the fledgling stage.

Seeking to improve those odds in 1976, the researchers mounted the nesting boxes on aluminum poles, then applied axle grease and hot pepper to the supports. With this system, the percentage of survivors nearly doubled in the following two summers.

Morton and Snyder plan to report their successful technique to the North American Bluebird Society so that others can try it. They also intend to employ a new box design that, in addition, will discourage sparrows and starlings.

While an important and practical piece of conservation biology, this work has no striking implications for the Zoo, at least on the surface. In the long run, however, it may prevent yet another beautiful, indigenous bird from taking up final residence in a small reserve, a zoo cage—or on a museum shelf.

Local field work like this bluebird study provides excellent training for young re-

In a pose belying its aggressive nature, a chipmunk savors sunflower seeds from a backyard bird feeder in a Connecticut suburb.

searchers earning advanced degrees in zoology. Expert supervision lies close at hand, and the logistics of the study are more manageable if research can be done in rural Maryland or Virginia, rather than Madagascar or Malaysia.

A second study along those same lines, partially funded and supervised by the Office of Zoological Research, revealed heretofore hidden truths about another common creature, the frisky, striped Eastern chipmunk, also called ground squirrel.

Both common and active during the daytime, this small squirrel might seem a poor, that is, over-studied, choice for a new project. But no one had really taken a thorough look at its social and foraging behavior until student Lang Elliot came along. He chose a two-acre plot of forested land in the Adirondacks of upstate New York, and then devised a clever observational tool for his study: a portable lifeguard tower. Above him each day arched a leafy canopy of beech, maple, yellow birch, and spruce trees, while below scampered dozens of chipmunks.

These animals are solitary, aggressive, and intolerant little creatures that spend much of their time locked in a miniature rendition of king-of-the-mountain. Each animal lives alone in an intricately excavated burrow with a central nest and several food storage chambers. Elliot soon observed that a chipmunk is absolutely humorless about the 40 to 50 feet of land surrounding its burrow.

That territory is his to forage, and the casual intruder is chased vigorously from the premises—the closer to the burrow, the more vigorous the chase. These territorial squabbles can be wild affairs with zigzagging runs, aerial somersaults, and role reversals wherein the chaser becomes the chased and heads for his burrow. Only in the demilitarized zones between home territories do chipmunks tolerate each other.

Foraging space is critical to chipmunks because their winter survival depends on stores of seeds and nuts. Early one October, Elliot watched a single adult carry 25 cheek pouchfuls of beech nuts (25 nuts per load) to her burrow in a three-hour period. At this rate, by the end of fall, her food hoard would have contained 15,000 to 20,000 nuts and seeds!

Despite their aggressiveness, chipmunks aren't completely asocial, and Elliot was able to observe two group activities: "chucking" and mating. When a predator such as a hawk flew by, Elliot saw the chipmunks freeze in place and begin, almost in unison, to make a "chucking" sound like hoofs clomping on dry pavement. Since many of the chipmunks are at least distantly related, the action could be interpreted as genetic altruism—relatives helping each other to survive. But the more immediate and practical explanation for this mysterious group surveillance is that it tells the predator: "We see you, so you might as well give up." This in turn allows the chipmunks to recommence their foraging, rather than run for their burrows.

Chipmunk mating turned out to be a frantic affair, during which eight to 10 males, lured by an estrous female's scent, would converge on her territory and chase her back and forth until, in the end, she allowed a male to catch her. In his research paper, Elliot dubbed this group courting ritual a "mating bout"—but in private he calls it a "mob scene."

This chipmunk reconnaissance became Elliot's graduate thesis and, says one of his supervisors, Eugene Morton, it prepared him for a lifetime of zoological study. Some of that will have direct practical relevance to the captive animals of the National Zoo. And some will have theoretical importance for the field of zoology. Although tame compared to, say, tiger studies in Nepal, it was an altogether appropriate project for the Office of Zoological Research. "In a sense," Dr. Morton says, "the Smithsonian is the nation's university. And one of its prime missions is to gather and disseminate knowledge, in one form or another." □

BUILD YOUR OWN BLUEBIRD NESTING BOX

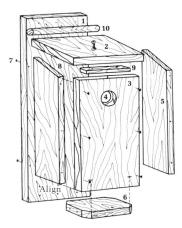

1 Back: 5½ x 16½ inches

2 Top: 6½ x 7 inches. Dowel and cleat help position removable top, which is secured by 1½-inch wood screw with washer

3 Front: 5½ x 9⅞ inches

4 Entrance hole: precisely 1½ inches in diameter, 1⅛ inches from top

5 Sides 4 x 10¾ inches (back edge) and 9¾ inches (front edge)

6 Bottom: 4 x 4 inches. Cut corners off bottom for drainage; recess bottom ¼ inch

7 Use 1¾-inch galvanized siding nails or aluminum nails

8 Space between top and sides allows ventilation

9 Cleat

10 Dowel

Use ¾-inch boards

Plans for a predator-proof bluebird nesting box, above, have helped the Conservation and Research Center's successful program, below.

ZEBRAS IN VIRGINIA?

A FUTURE FOR ANIMALS

Amy Donovan

Route 522 winds through a picturesque section of Virginia's Shenandoah Valley, stark and quiet late one February day. Despite the countryside's aura of hibernation, however, a startled motorist might well glimpse a herd of zebras on a nearby hillside. The highway cuts through the National Zoo's 3,150-acre Conservation and Research Center outside Front Royal, a sleepy town known as the starting point for breathtaking automobile trips over the crest of the Blue Ridge Mountains. Under Smithsonian auspices only since 1975, this exotic animal breeding farm 75 miles west of Washington has already made its mark in international zoological circles.

The Center's curious assortment of buildings recalls a military base, albeit an odd one: two water reservoirs, row houses and a dormitory, barns, and a huge granary loom up in the frosty air. One of the largest conservation and breeding centers for exotic animals in the United States, its most striking aspect is its spaciousness, the essential ingredient for the often complex process of breeding exotics in captivity. Pastures and woodlands roll away from the central compound, accommodating the numerous herds of ungulates, or hoofed stock, all of which are for the most part free to roam within large fenced pastures. With the staff's help, the tropical species—zebras, Eld's deer, and oryxes—have acclimated to life in the temperate zone.

Meanwhile, in other areas of the Center, the lesser pandas' breeding season has begun. The rufous-and-black males pace nervously around their large outdoor corn cribs, while the females peer out from their nest boxes. In a valley nearby, gray sandhill cranes in individual yards throw back their heads and pour forth their loud, haunting call, evocative of an Everglades marsh.

Beginning in the late 1700s, homesteaders cleared much of the thick woodlands that once covered this area, building cabins and farming the scenic hillsides. Then, in 1909, the Army bought up 42 farms and established a breeding and training center for cavalry horses and mules. A gravity-flow water transport system still supplies water to the central compound from mountain springs over two miles away. A K-9 Corps unit and a German prisoner-of-war camp operated on

Staff members break ice along a fence in the muntjac yard, opposite top, so that the small tropical deer can gain traction. Research observation tower is at upper right. Below: Bactrian camels, scimitar-horned oryx, and a Persian onager.

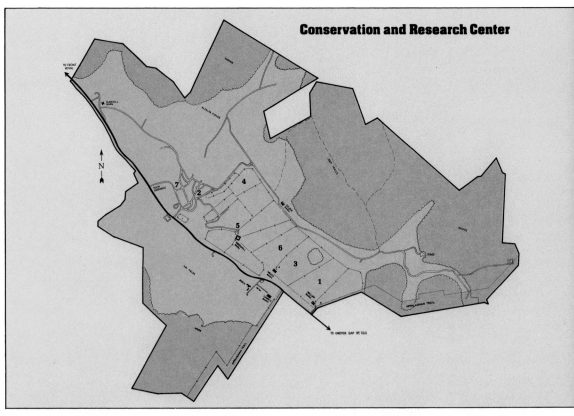

Conservation and Research Center

A map, top, shows the location of some of the animals at Front Royal. Corresponding to the map's numbers are, from left to right: top row, Grant's zebra (1), lesser panda (2), Eld's deer (3), and wisent (4); middle row, emu (5); and bottom row, Bactrian camel (6), and maned wolf (7).

the site during World War II, after which the U.S. Department of Agriculture took over, launching extensive research projects on beef cattle production for the next 25 years.

When Agriculture pulled out in 1974, the Zoo went after this acreage, in Director Reed's words, "like a starving tiger downwind of a sleeping buffalo." Issued a temporary permit, the Zoo began fencing and moved in animals and personnel as soon as possible. Dr. Reed sought to establish the Zoo's presence by having the place so overrun with animals and Zoo signs on buildings and equipment that other agencies would feel rather put off from trying to obtain the land.

Reed's efforts finally paid off, and in July 1975 the already well-entrenched National Zoo officially took charge of the Front Royal property, built more fencing, and inaugurated one of its most important activities in the latter half of this century.

* * *

On a clear, sub-freezing morning Jim Murtaugh, the lead keeper of the Center's more than 100 ungulates, and Kevin Conway, another keeper, set off in a jeep to feed and check on the herds. First stop, the zebras.

Murtaugh and Conway can tell by the tracks in the snow that the zebras have been very active. Only now, after several months in this pasture, have these natives of the savanna begun to go up into the woods in search of forage, playing a virtual cat-and-mouse game with the tropical Eld's deer from Burma, cohabitants of the zebras' large enclosure. The herd has discovered the deer's favorite area of honeysuckle, a good forage plant that keeps its leaves throughout most of the winter, and the shy deer have retreated farther into the brush. Yet Murtaugh has seen the zebras and the deer eating together at the same place, an uncharacteristic display of tolerance on the part of the instinctively aggressive striped horses.

Since female zebras remain fertile throughout the year, the male is removed and kept separate from the herd from September through March. Like all horses, zebras give birth after an 11-month gestation period, and a female could not both lactate and keep herself warm if she delivered in the winter. The low temperatures would also place severe strain on the offspring. When the stallion is reintroduced to the herd in the spring, all the females generally conceive in the same time period, making zebra births the next year considerably easier for keepers to handle.

In addition to the herd of six mares and one stallion, two foals were born in the spring of 1978 and one was expected in the spring of 1979. Not endangered like the Hartman's Mountain or Grevy's zebra, explains Murtaugh, a successful program with the Plains zebra would allow the Center to take on one of the rarer, more threatened horse species at a later time. That is why the Center's current pilot study of the Plains zebra is so important.

No road leads up from the zebras' barn to either of the two feeding stations which the keepers maintain for the Eld's deer, so the jeep crisscrosses and slip-slides its way up the slick, snowy hillside to the woods. In the summer, thick foliage offers security to these secretive forest dwellers. Currently, a brand new Eld's deer breeding complex allows the staff greater latitude in effectively managing these extremely flighty animals. Six paddocks funnel directly into three buildings, so that keepers and others can maintain a distance when attempting to herd the deer indoors. In their natural wild state, the Eld's deer practically self-destruct with panic when confined and when keepers attempt to catch them for routine checkups.

Murtaugh and Conway return to the jeep after searching in vain for the tropical deer, finally having to be content with studying their hoof prints in the snow. A double set of fencing and gates secures the entrances into the pastures, an extra precaution against an animal slipping out past the keeper.

Seldom publicized, the Center is neither a zoo nor a safari park, as it is not designed around the idea of public animal exhibits. An integral part of the Zoo, Front Royal is closely tied to and shares Rock Creek's staff, facilities, and scientific research. The Center does not study threatened species exclusively, but includes Zoo exhibit ones as well. For example, although Bactrian camels serve as beasts of burden in Asia, and wild populations still exist in Mongolia, they have been infrequently bred in this country. For this reason, in part, two breeding herds have been established at Front Royal, where their behavior is under close scrutiny.

Wisent, or European bison, roam the pastures adjacent to the camels. They are no longer extinct in the wild, as offspring from captive stocks have been reintroduced to natural habitats. While the stocky, powerful animals are forest-dwelling, as opposed to our plains-dwelling American buffalo, their behavior in captivity closely resembles that of domestic cattle.

One bachelor onager, or Asiatic wild ass, mingles with the wisent, while two others pace nearby in separate pastures. Typical of adult male behavior in many horse species, these dun-colored onagers seem to thrive on aggression and would fight year round if given the chance. Because of the onagers' belligerent dispositions, curators are seeking to separate each male by at least one intervening pasture. Now the horses often engage in fence running, pursuing each other testily up and down their chain-link boundary.

Joel Berger, a postdoctoral student, is studying dominance hierarchies among the Center's Persian onagers, a particular subspecies that comes from a part of Iran whose winter climate resembles that at Front Royal. The mares, like the stallions, exhibit a high degree of aggression, setting up strict matriarchies which often hold sway even over the males.

After a mid-morning coffee break, Murtaugh and Conway receive help from several other keepers in supplying baled alfalfa and a commercial feed to the Père David's deer and the scimitar-horned oryxes, the first two species to be kept at the Center. The deer had been known to the Chinese for centuries and were already extinct in the wild when Father Armand David, a French priest, came upon a herd of them in 1865 in Peking's Imperial Hunting Park. The females at Front Royal, now accustomed to feeding in a fenced-in area, are easier to manage in the winter because the staff controls their food supply.

After a strenuous morning of feeding and checking on all the hoofed stock, Murtaugh and his fellow keepers can look forward to spending the afternoon cleaning out one of the barns, another manifestation of a markedly increased winter workload. The chain-link pasture fences often shrink in the cold, necessitating vigorous adjustments of the bars and padlocks. Snow makes driving and trudging to the animals more difficult. Keepers must carry range supplements to the ungulates daily, break up the ice in their water troughs, and clean out their barns once a week. Yet the workers carry out these ostensibly thankless tasks with a strong sense of professionalism, duty, and concern for the animals, proving themselves, as Curator-in-charge Chris Wemmer commented, the fundamental element in a zoo.

As Front Royal's curator of mammals, Larry Collins oversees 189 animals and numerous breeding and research programs. The satellite breeding operation involving the golden lion marmosets, for example, supplements Rock Creek's in-depth study and has enjoyed similar success.

Unable to withstand the cold, the marmosets winter in a building equipped with temperature and humidity controls. They spend summers outdoors, bounding about the branches in their spacious cages.

In another building are 11 buff-furred Matschie's tree kangaroos, the biggest group in captivity outside of their native New Guinea, where they inhabit only the Huon Peninsula (see page 177). They creep slowly along the branches in their winter quarters, their long yellow tails serving as balance poles. These crepuscular vegetarians have been known to jump or fall 30 feet from limbs in their cages, however, and the staff has therefore covered the floor of their outdoor enclosures with astroturf.

After approximately only a 30-day gestation period, female tree kangaroos give birth to lima bean-sized embryos. The tiny newborns work their way into the mother's pouch, not to emerge until they can voluntarily release the mother's nipple from their mouths. Because it is almost impossible to verify a tree kangaroo birth until a marked swelling appears in the mother's pouch, Collins is working with some of the female tree kangaroos, trying to tame them to the point where he can check their pouches regularly and thus pinpoint the precise date of a birth.

Another ongoing study in the mammals division involves pair-bonding in bush dogs, short-legged, coarse-haired animals from the tropical forests of South America. Ingrid Porton, a doctoral student studying monogamy in canids under the direction of Devra Kleiman at the Zoo, is working with a pair that have produced the second captive bush dog litter at the Center, although only one female pup survived the first birth.

The males play a role in the reproductive process that appears unique, at least in a canine species. At birth, Porton explains, the male assists in helping to pull the puppies out of the mother. Then, perhaps as an endocrine function, he devours much of the afterbirth. As is usual for carnivorous female animals, the mother also eats some of the afterbirth, which may stimulate lactation. Curiously, the female bush dog emits loud calls at birth, whereas most female animals instinc-

The Center's staff collaborate on animal enclosure designs. At top, a grounds crew staff member welds a fence for the maned wolves' pens. Ingrid Porton, left, a graduate researcher, consults with carpenter Lowane Johnson about installing entries for the canids she is studying. Above, keeper Ken Lang adapts a corn crib for the clouded leopards.

tively give birth quietly, safeguarding themselves at a vulnerable moment.

Guy Greenwell, Front Royal's curator of birds, has kept wild birds for over 55 years. Today, he keeps scores of cranes, threatened tropical parrots and songbirds, and both hardy and large flightless birds. To visit his office in the basement of the administration building is to become immediately engulfed in the Center's—and to a great extent the world's—bird husbandry program. Bird photographs and unique feathers occupy strategic positions around the room, while intricate building plans for proposed bird yards, many of them drawn by Greenwell himself, rest on the two drafting tables.

The Center's bird program began somewhat curiously. In 1975, because of heavy, disruptive construction in the Bird House in Rock Creek Park, tropical or tender species of birds came to Front Royal for what was then considered only a temporary visit. As the visit proved a success, and since the Zoo had never been able to provide enough room for breeding and rearing its birds, Dr. Reed and others quickly began to visualize a permanent bird-breeding program at the Center.

Keeper Bobby Rodden, top left, looks out over a Darwin's rhea to the scimitar-horned oryx. Below left, a seated rhea. These large, flightless birds, like the emu below, here with a young Eld's deer, share paddocks with certain hoofed stock.

Many bird species fail to produce well in captivity, often extending little effort toward rearing their young. Certain kinds of birds must therefore be artificially incubated and reared, and these form the backbone of Greenwell's and the Center's efforts. Those birds that rear their young well in captivity are left alone, for, as Greenwell explains, "We're striving toward natural rather than artificial breeding, one possible goal being reintroduction to the wild."

The 21 recently finished crane yards illustrate the Center's attention to its prime focus of breeding animals. Each large yard has a running stream, a marsh, a water system to rejuvenate the marsh, and a small aluminum shed with an electric panel for heating. Greenwell and his assistants hang feeders in these sheds in order to help the birds overcome their fear of being enclosed so that they will learn to use the shelters during the cold weather. Although no crane has yet been attacked by one of its resident natural enemies —great-horned owls, bobcats, raccoons— a special outer "predator fence" surrounds each pen.

The large, flightless birds, such as the emus and the Darwin's rhea, will continue to live as they have with the hoofed stock, whose pastures and barns suit them.

The current major bird effort involves the building and stocking of hardy-bird yards, enclosures for birds such as mountain-dwelling pheasants that can withstand the weather. Greenwell also foresees rehabilitating some small buildings for semi-hardy birds. When the first hardy-bird yards are completed and stocked, perhaps in the late fall of 1979, Greenwell will turn his attention to two other projects: a small mammal/delicate bird complex with indoor and outdoor quarters; and accommodations for several special groups of birds, including colony breeders such as ibis that would require heated shelter.

Bird incubating and rearing efforts take place in a renovated building that houses such important equipment as antique-looking redwood-and-glass incubators, in which eggs are placed after they have been collected and numbered; special boxes for infant waterfowl, each with a heat lamp directly over it; cages for waterfowl chicks, complete with electrically heated floors around each miniature pool; and enclosures for yearling birds, with outdoor sections for use in summer months. Each bird is color-banded immediately after hatching, enabling keepers or managers to keep track of individuals' growth and establish accurate genealogy lines.

With the Center's housing space at a premium during this building phase, the bird program's tropical breeding pairs currently share a section of another building with the golden marmosets. Carolyn Emerick, the lead bird keeper, is studying the behavior of Rothschild's mynahs, striking blue-and-white birds. The other breeding species are the Bornean great argus pheasant, the crested quail dove, and the near-extinct Grand Cayman Amazon parrot.

Greenwell and Emerick know there remains much to do in completing the Center's avian research and breeding programs. This work, like that with other animals, rotates on a seasonal basis. Bird egg-laying and rearing of the young occur in the spring and the summer, a time when construction, such as that which must be completed on the hardy-bird yards, moves ahead faster. As Greenwell explains it, "We are not in production in the winter." And yet in referring only to outdoor or actual bird-rearing activities, he is modestly omitting all the important work accomplished during the cold months. While snow blankets the ground, Emerick maintains records as all keepers must, collating data on avian health and behavior, while Greenwell initiates and carries out other long-term projects. He has sent other zoos his questionnaire on the tropical Rothschild's mynahs, for example, in order to begin an inter-zoo communication network of genealogy lines.

As the days begin to lengthen, pregnant zebra and onager mares edge ever closer to their delivery days in the spring. The incubators in Building 5 continue to hum, stirring more life into their diverse assembly of eggs with each rotation of the drum. A bloodied male yearling crane, a victim of its own species' severe aggressiveness, recuperates in a holding cage. And curators and keepers wait anxiously to see whether Mishka, a female clouded leopard, will mate with the chosen male cat; and whether all four bush dog puppies will survive to adulthood. Life, with all its offsetting ramifications, is the name of the game at the Zoo's Conservation and Research Center.

The breeding function of zoos has become imperative, and the Front Royal facility, while not unique in its goals, surely holds a strategic place in the future of many of the world's threatened animals. □

A renovated granary, far left, now serves as the Center's commissary, where keepers prepare food for the animals. Parked nearby is an old army surplus ambulance, now specially outfitted to transport sick animals. The rolls of new fence wire in the foreground indicate how important fencing is at Front Royal. Top, a white-tailed deer jumps an old 4-foot cattle fence. Lower left, Grant's zebras feed from troughs first used by cavalry horses. Left, zebras rub noses, a common greeting among this species.

DOWN ON THE FARM

The pastures may hold Persian onagers instead of golden Guernseys, European wisent instead of Black Angus; and raucous tropical songbirds are a far cry from bantams. Yet the Conservation and Research Center's staff watches its potential breeders as carefully as any diligent farmer. Indeed, as the Front Royal breeding farm is keeping many species about which little is known, curators, keepers, and researchers often must start from scratch in accumulating information on the Center's animals. Curators oversee research into animal behavior and social organization in order primarily to establish management schemes and husbandry methods for the Center's exotic animals, and ultimately to help conserve threatened species.

For the hoofed stock, the most numerous animals on Front Royal's vast acreage, Chris Wemmer, curator-in-charge, stresses the importance of setting up balanced age-distribution pyramids. Each herd is consciously structured with an eye to age, seemingly an easy proposition. In fact, however, many difficulties arise when a zoologist attempts to control such natural demographic variables as age-specific mortality, dispersal, and recruitment. One year, for example, five of the 10 females in a herd may be producing young. On the other hand, if three will likely stop producing in a year, should they be sent away? Will another zoo accept any or all of them? Can female replacements be found?

Productivity, then, dictates effective age structure in herds. Obviously, Zoo personnel must avoid allowing all the animals in a herd to go post-productive at the same time. Also, the closer the animals are in age, the more strife and dominance hierarchy problems result. In seeking to even out the social rela-

Keeper Jim Murtaugh, silhouetted in the doorway of one of the Front Royal barns, pours pelleted feed, a supplement for the hoofed stock, most all of which receive adequate nutrients from grazing. Come winter, bales of hay and alfalfa, stored from the summer's crop, serve as further dietary supplements to help the animals ready themselves for the cold. Those that don't grow heavy coats put on a layer of fat. The Center raises enough hay during good seasons to feed all its animals and many of those at the Zoo proper, no small saving in the face of dramatically rising feed costs.

tionships among the animals, curators feed
one or two offspring and some of the post-
productive adults back into the herd and
then try to arrange breeding loans for the
surplus animals.

Père David's deer, for example, have lived
at Front Royal for over four years, and the
herd is just now approaching a viable structure. The Center got the deer on breeding
loans from several sources, trying to obtain
animals as distantly related as possible. The
staff then shipped out the nonproducers and,
as the herd started producing young and thus
increasing, began to sort ages, sending near-
post-productive females out and feeding in
new animals. Dr. Wemmer predicts it will be
10 or 12 more years before the deer, through
painstaking human management, reach an
optimum age distribution.

The Père David's harem system, unlike that
of some ungulates, ensures fairly clear-cut
parentage records. When both male and
female deer live together in the same pasture,
one stag establishes himself as herd master.
For the next six weeks or so, this male deer
will eat and sleep very little, obsessed with
excluding other males and with impregnat-
ing those females in estrus. Finally, fatigued
and gaunt, he will lose his place, usually
after a fight, to another stag who then, for the
length of his "rule," becomes the sole im-
pregnating male. As further corroboration to
this system, the staff has witnessed about 85
percent of all fertile copulations.

A Front Royal study that grew directly
from research at the Zoo in Washington involves golden lion marmosets. Fifteen of the
diminutive monkeys live here in three family
groups, and one female has raised two sets of
triplets, only the second and third times a
female has reared such a large litter in captivity. Although marmosets do occasionally
bear triplets, captive mothers usually raise

**Male Père David's deer, right, at pasture. The two
at left are sparring. Opposite top, artist Lucia de
Leiris works on an illustration for Curator-in-
charge Chris Wemmer's forthcoming book on the
deer. Below, her sketch of a suckling calf.**

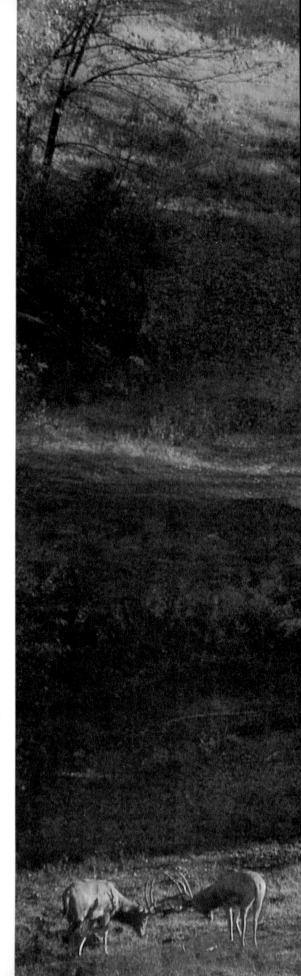

only two of the young, since the normal litter size is one or two. Studies of their family dynamics and structure tie in with pair-bonding studies of three canids—maned wolves, bush dogs, and crab-eating foxes—another project which Reproduction Zoologist Devra Kleiman organized.

Melissa Ditton, pictured at right observing marmoset behavior, is a biotechnician with the Zoo's Office of Zoological Research, assigned to Front Royal to assist with some of that office's continuing studies. This particular set of photographs of Ditton at work actually depicts a somewhat atypical situation. Marmalade, the monkey she is studying, was placed in an incubator as an infant because of a problem with her parents, and then was hand reared by humans. Completely tame, the marmoset will not hesitate to cavort with those she knows particularly well. For this reason, Ditton generally observes Marmalade and the other marmosets inside their building so that she can watch from a walkway outside the cage area. It is difficult to make observations, she points out, when the monkey is climbing on her shoulders.

The clipboard and attached timer are the sine qua non of Ditton's and others' golden marmoset observations. She notes information on marmoset data sheets which Dr. Kleiman devised for recording the activities and interactions of adult pairs, juveniles, and infants. The data sheets break down further into behaviors particular to different age groups. Contact behavior for adults, for example, encompasses marmoset reactions during their encounters, and the participants in and duration of wrestling and huddling activities. Grooming behavior is noted among all ages, while chasing applies only to juveniles and infants.

One of the most interesting and least understood behaviors is that of marking, rare among infants. Golden marmosets have glands on their chests that secrete a substance for marking branches and other objects. Genital secretions serve the same function. Ditton and others have observed that, among juveniles, one may mark a good deal more and more often than others, and the researchers wonder whether this could imply a dominance trait.

Competition between juveniles to carry infants is keen. When one wishes to carry a particular infant, it approaches and situates itself over the infant, pressing its chest over the baby so it can climb on. Juveniles tend to

Melissa Ditton, a Zoo researcher assigned to Front Royal, observes Marmalade, an incubator- and hand-reared golden marmoset. Far right, Marmalade huddles with another marmoset.

take over some baby-carrying duties after the infant's first few weeks, and then the mother begins to carry less and less, and the father and the juveniles more and more.

Front Royal has proven so far to be an ideal place to carry out the Zoo's canid studies. One of the Center's breeding breakthroughs, for example, is the maned wolf, a high-strung animal of the Brazilian savanna that would most likely succumb to stress in an urban zoo environment. Chuck Brady, a doctoral student who worked with bush dogs, crab-eating foxes, and maned wolves, devised a format for breeding the wolves in captivity. His management criteria for the pregnant wolves brought considerable success: three litters have been born at the Center and reared by their mothers, rare events in the history of this species' captivity.

Here, in rural Virginia, the wolves find the quiet and the spacious grassy pens they need, and researchers have not had to invade their privacy to gather information. Instead, Brady set up isolated dens and closed-circuit TV monitors so that researchers can note behavior, particularly at such critical times as birth and pup rearing, without intruding into the wolves' and the other canids' dens.

The Center is establishing standard hatching and growth data on Stanley, Indian sarus, and Florida sandhill cranes. Each female crane usually lays two eggs per clutch. To increase the number of cranes that can be raised, keepers pull eggs from the nest for incubation, as evolution has endowed the female crane with the curious ability to recycle and lay another clutch, generally 12 to 18 days later. Although female cranes have been known to lay 14 eggs a season through this method, and the number varies by crane pair, at Front Royal they usually produce eight. Keepers pull just one of the female's last clutch, both to allow her to raise one chick and to keep the older baby crane from killing the younger one, behavior that occurs extensively in cranes.

To avoid having the birds imprint on

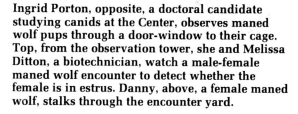

Ingrid Porton, opposite, a doctoral candidate studying canids at the Center, observes maned wolf pups through a door-window to their cage. Top, from the observation tower, she and Melissa Ditton, a biotechnician, watch a male-female maned wolf encounter to detect whether the female is in estrus. Danny, above, a female maned wolf, stalks through the encounter yard.

humans, keepers place two crane eggs in a hatcher with a wire divider. That way the chicks can see and communicate with each other from their earliest moments. Further, in order to ensure that the young cranes learn their species' sexual behavior and therefore eventually become breeders, they are put with adult cranes whenever possible before they are half feathered.

Frank Kohn, another researcher at the Center, is working with binturongs, or Asian bear cats. The largest of the civet family, the binturong is also the only Old World carnivore with a prehensile tail.

Civets rely on smell, and perhaps for this reason have developed large, musk-producing perineal scent glands between their rear legs. It is just this gland that Kohn, under the direction of Chris Wemmer, is studying. In females, the gland connects with the vagina and secretes a heavy, relatively mild fatty substance. Dr. Wemmer, Kohn, and others are trying to discover the chemical components of this secretion. Is it a directly scented product, or does it become the carrying matrix for a scent generated in the reproductive tract? Musk amplifies or exalts scents mixed with it, and so perhaps serves to exaggerate or

Carolyn Emerick, top, checks pair of sandhill cranes. Particularly assertive during breeding season, male attacks Emerick, opposite; male sarus crane does same, above and below.

broadcast the civet's sexual hormones.

Once Wemmer and his assistants have figured out precisely the nature of this substance and how it works, they will seek to discover how it aids the binturong in its natural environment. An arboreal dweller in thick forests that allow only limited visual contact, binturongs may communicate with one another through scent codes. The tests which Kohn is conducting with the animals may illustrate the amount of information and the degree of discrimination carried in the scents, how specific the identification process is, and whether a scent announces not just which binturong it is, but its physical condition and sexual receptivity as well.

The Tariff Act of 1930 prohibited the importation of domestic animals from any countries where foot-and-mouth and certain other diseases are endemic. Faced some 20 years later with the prospect of losing Bactrian camels as exhibit animals, Dr. Reed initiated reproductive and behavioral studies of the Zoo's Bactrian camels to ensure their continued presence in American zoos.

Male camels can impregnate females only during the stallions' rutting period, which occurs in late winter in Virginia. At this time of year, a gland at the back of the male camel's skull secretes a redolent substance with which the animal marks or scents its

Frank Kohn, top, feeds a binturong a banana, its favorite fruit, as part of his attempt to familiarize the animals to him. Left, Abraham, a male binturong now familiar with the researcher, confronts Kohn nose to nose, and, above, allows him to take a sample of perineal gland secretion with a cotton swab. At center top, Kohn presents scent-coded fingers to a binturong in a separate enclosure, measuring degree of interest and amount of time spent examining the scents in an olfactory manner. Kohn collates data on the olfactory communication behavior of the Center's binturongs, opposite.

front hump and which it rubs on surrounding objects, thus delineating its territory. The stallions also engage in urine-flicking, using their tails both to saturate their rear humps with urine and to fling some of the liquid around the immediate area.

Female Bactrians reproduce once every two years and then only one calf at a time. In order to understand this performance better, the Center intends to have a doctoral research program carried out on seasonal hormone cycles of males and females to correlate hormone changes and levels with behavior.

As the Bactrian camels have become acclimated to Front Royal's rolling pastures and thus supplied researchers with information on herd dynamics and exotic animal range management, so other little-understood animals have provided data on different aspects of exotic animal husbandry. Space—from the crane yards to the maned wolves' enclosures to the hoofed stock paddocks—has proven invaluable to the Center's scientific research and concurrent attempt to sustain the gene pools of exotic wildlife. □

Dirty Mary, top right, one of Front Royal's 16 Bactrian camels, nuzzles keeper Dave Shifflett; mare stands with offspring, center. Keeper Bobby Rodden checks camel, below, and, opposite, two Bactrians graze in autumn light.

SECTION IV
ZOO AMERICA

DIFFERENT CLIMATES

DIFFERENT ZOOS

John F. Eisenberg

It can be read by the telling way early man rendered the beasts in his life on cave walls: he knew the anatomy and habits of those animals intimately. Indeed, where he depended on hunting for a significant portion of his protein intake, it was this very knowledge of wildlife behavior that ensured his survival. But when human settlements became more permanent, simple forms of codified land use arose with respect to both animals and plants. More and more, cultural economics, social customs, even class stratification determined who could avail himself of what, and how much. For example, as such early civilizations grew, royalty tended to retain hunting privileges exclusively for itself and for the associated nobility. Rather than a form of subsistence, therefore, game animals became a mechanism for maintaining the skills of the aristocratic hunter. It was no accident that such skills were approximately the same as those required in warfare, the traditional trade of the high-born.

Gradually, the forests and preserves evolved from private "wilderness" areas to fenced enclosures stocked with managed herds. The land on which the London zoo now stands in Regents Park, for example, was once part of a royal hunting preserve. Nor was the practice of managing game animals in large enclosures—for the benefit of the few—peculiar to the West. It also had a long history in China.

Another tradition germane to the formation of zoos evolved independently of the hunt and the herds managed solely for sport. Collections of live and often exotic animals were maintained as curiosities by the rulers of many early civilizations. As many as 3,000 years ago one of the Chinese emperors sup-

Siberian tigers tussle in the snow at the Calgary zoo. Reflecting a recent trend, the zoo is designing exhibits around climate.

The San Diego Wild Animal Park's success in breeding African white rhinoceroses has helped save the species from extinction. It is larger than its counterpart, the black rhino.

ported such a collection—for the stated purpose of "enlightenment"—perhaps illustrating some of the more sublime seeds of man's impulse to create zoos.

But the modern zoological garden took its more familiar shape during the rise of industrial civilization in Western Europe. By an early modern zoological park I mean something more than a casual menagerie assembled for the entertainment of the public: rather, a repository for exotic specimens of animal life to be studied as a way of understanding the fauna and flora of those areas of the globe that had recently come under the influence of Western Europe.

Zoological parks, incidentally, developed independently from botanical gardens. Plants have always been economically important, and early botanical gardens often rose in association with universities or centers of learning. A botanical collection, moreover, obviously involved less demanding care and expense than an exotic animal collection.

It was not until public monies—rather than royal stipends—started supporting zoological study collections that the modern zoo truly came into being. The prototype was the zoological garden at Regents Park, established by the Zoological Society of London in 1826.

From the beginning, the collection at London was to be studied in order to elucidate the natural history of exotic living animals. Appropriate veterinary care and postmortems also became necessary not only to keep the animals alive, but to learn something from their deaths. Furthermore, deceased specimens could be turned over to the British Museum (Natural History) for preservation and even later study. In this way the denizens of the then expanding British Empire could be named, classified, and assessed with respect to their potential contribution to knowledge.

This sort of enterprise was a far cry from a royal menagerie which might be maintained for the entertainment of the king and his court, albeit that such menageries often furnished materials for national museums. It was the purpose behind the London charter that set a new tone: namely, to collect exotic animals, to keep them healthy, to study them, and, finally, to determine cause of death.

During the Industrial Revolution, great centers of wealth rose in the northern hemisphere, whose explorers and colonizers traveled for the most part to the tropics. The result was that artificial life support systems had to be devised for the exotic birds, mam-

Animal collections have been documented in many ancient civilizations. The Chinese created game parks where royalty could hunt, as depicted in this 17th-century painting.

mals, and reptiles brought to northern climates. Of necessity the exhibit areas tended to be set in buildings that could be heated during the temperate-zone winter. Rather than outdoor exhibits, zoos constructed massive indoor aviaries and exotic mammal houses, only occasionally fencing outside yards where tropical specimens might be exhibited during the warm months.

The idea of maintaining exotic specimens with the object of studying the natural history of animals found in remote parts of the world—as well as studying associated factors, such as tropical diseases—soon spread from London throughout Western Europe. In the United States, zoological gardens with similar aims became established in various cities. Philadelphia lays claim to forming the first zoological society in America, and its zoo is among the oldest in the country. Facing similar climatic problems, it too followed the pattern set by London, erecting large heated houses to carry its exotic specimens through the winter. New York soon followed suit. Although the city kept a menagerie in

Central Park, it set aside a vast tract in the then underdeveloped Bronx and, in addition to erecting the necessary housing for exotics, created spacious paddocks. Shortly after, new zoological parks also sprang up in St. Louis and Chicago.

Because industrialization in the United States proceeded from the Northeast to the Midwest, the constraints of climate influenced the early design of these parks just as they had those in Europe. Massive houses with adjoining yards served pachyderms such as rhinoceroses, hippopotamuses, and elephants. Ornate, steam-heated reptile houses with a series of glass-fronted cages displayed reptiles and tropical amphibians. The hardier forms of North American fauna, of course, could roam in more spacious outdoor enclosures. This was especially true of such forms as the American bison which, when threatened with extinction, was maintained by the New York Zoological Society in the large paddocks in the Bronx. In fact, it was with the aim of conserving endangered ungulates in the United States that acreage was originally set aside in Rock Creek Park. The site became a focal point that eventually led to the formation of the National Zoo in Washington, D.C.

Even with the best of intentions of conserving endangered species or providing a place to study exotic vertebrates, from the outset most zoos had to face the need to support themselves. If a zoo were operated by a zoological society, the society itself was dependent on some form of income, since even the most ardent donors could not have been expected to bear the total financial burden. But if admission were charged, then very soon zoos had to confront the fact that the public had tastes that didn't always coincide with the lofty scientific goals of the founding societies. At the same time, zoos encountered stiff competition from other organizations which pandered to the spectacular and bizarre. As a result, zoological gardens often found themselves straying from the aims of conservation and scientific inquiry, creating instead, in a setting resembling something between a deer park and a circus, a side-show atmosphere. This was especially true in the United States, where traveling menageries had always been popular and received wide public support, particularly in rural areas that could not generate sufficient revenues to

Ringling Brothers and Barnum & Bailey Circus poster exalts the show's exotic animals.

Line between zoo and carnival remains blurred, as exemplified in this marine mammal show.

establish their own permanent collections. American zoos were founded during the era of P. T. Barnum, and it clearly showed. Barnum's goal, after all, was to make money, pure and simple. And it was he who coined the phrase, "There's a sucker born every minute." It took zoos a long time to extricate themselves from the more extreme manifestations of that carnival atmosphere.

Meanwhile, fortunately, more significant trends took shape, including the aesthetics of animal exhibition which, again, received great impetus from Europe. The Hagenbeck family in Hamburg had amassed a considerable fortune in the animal trade in those years. In the course of their business, they established an exhibition area that served both as a holding compound and as a source of income since visitors paid admission. As the popularity of their enterprise grew, the Hagenbecks began to experiment with a new type of exhibitry, dispensing with bars and developing moated enclosures where the animals could roam before the public without intervening physical barriers. The method was particularly successful with large carni-

157

The Bronx zoo's African Plains was one of the first exhibits in this country designed to evoke a sense of wonder at the magnificence and diversity of animals in a natural setting.

vores and hoofed stock. The concepts developed by the Hagenbecks, widely copied in Europe, quickly spread to the United States and led to such notable exhibits as the African Plains at the Bronx, the moated enclosures in St. Louis and Chicago, and the spectacular development of the technique in one of the nation's first outdoor zoos, San Diego.

The rigors of climatic considerations, on the other hand, forced the zoos of the American Northeast and Midwest to effect a compromise between moated and spacious outdoor enclosures and indoor viewing areas, necessary for tropical vertebrates during the long cold winters.

After the First World War the London zoo once again played the role of a pioneer when it realized that the space necessary to maintain self-sustaining herds of hoofed stock simply was not available in the confines of Regents Park. At this time acreage was set aside some 70 kilometers to the north, in the hamlet of Whipsnade, to provide spacious paddocks for the propagation of herds of ungulates hardy enough to withstand the English winters. Enough space was allotted so that a large enough herd could be maintained

to prevent the deleterious effects of inbreeding and keep the breeding potential of the captive stock from declining. This foresighted concept is emulated by most zoos in the United States today. With the development of the Front Royal breeding farm, the National Zoological Park was able to realize a dream it had long nourished—a dream generated by the example of Whipsnade some 50 years before. The New York Zoological Society has also established a similar breeding farm in a more southerly clime on St. Catherines Island off the coast of Georgia.

As zoos matured during the 19th century, research generally fell under the guidance of a permanent curatorial staff. Historically, curators had access to, or joint appointments with, museums. Much of the early research, therefore, included basic descriptions of new specimens and their anatomy, a largely taxonomic exercise. Research efforts extended only gradually to studies on behavior, reproduction, and diet. In the United States, the Penrose Laboratories in Philadelphia began to take on the responsibility of developing improved diets for specimens in the city's collection. Some zoological parks also sponsored field research. In the early days, such research often involved trips by the curatorial staff both to study specimens and to procure them for their collection. The funding and operation of permanent field stations were pioneered by the New York Zoological Society which, for many years, sponsored a laboratory in Trinidad.

With an increasing commitment on the part of zoological gardens to conservation activities, zoos began to address themselves to the long-term captive propagation of endangered species. In order to sustain reproduction over many generations, certain applied studies were necessary, especially those touching on the outbreeding of captive populations to reduce the hazards of inbreeding depression. Inbreeding depression is the loss of fecundity resulting from the close crossing of relatives, a process well documented in the early part of the 20th century by agricultural researchers. To this end, the large breeding farms established in conjunction with metropolitan zoos have proved extremely useful. Although much pioneering research has been carried on by larger zoological parks, the smaller metropolitan zoos have also played an important role in such work. For example, smaller zoos have been instrumental in establishing programs involving original research on animal behavior, quite often carried out in conjunction with local colleges and universities. The success of these programs is attested to by the increasing number of contributions to professional journals describing observations made in small municipal zoos.

Although full-time veterinarians are a relatively recent addition to the permanent staffs of most zoos, biomedical research has always been an important adjunct of zoological parks, because keeping exotic specimens in captivity requires a basic understanding of nutrition and animal husbandry. In addition, the control of parasites and infectious diseases becomes critical when exotics are maintained in close confinement and where the spread of contagious diseases is an ever-present danger. Then there is appropriate postmortem work, which has contributed significantly to our knowledge of disease syndromes and their transmission. Recent attention to captive propagation, finally, involves learning the intricacies of reproduction. Indeed, the Zoological Society of London was instrumental in establishing laboratories devoted entirely to this subject.

Eastern screech owls, top, perch in the Bronx zoo's Color at Night exhibit, designed to show which part of the color spectrum nocturnal animals see. Above, a two-mile monorail carries visitors through the Bronx zoo's 38-acre Wild Asia.

All these historical, cultural, and scientific aspects notwithstanding, it is still climate that exerts the more profound influence on the daily life of a zoo. Driving down Rock Creek Parkway toward the National Zoo on an early day in November, I am impressed with the colors of the autumn leaves and unhappily realize that another season of leaf raking lies just ahead. With five white oaks in my back yard, the number of leaves which will drop is astounding, an interesting adaptation by deciduous trees to a period of the year when photosynthesis is no longer practical. All summer long the large broad leaves catch the sun's rays and convert carbon dioxide and water to sugars with an assist from light and the enzyme chlorophyll. But the onset of winter means the end of the

Contrary to appearances, this tiger at the Milwaukee zoo is unable to pounce on any of the herd below, its natural prey.

growing season. Temperatures will fall too low to permit rapid photosynthesis, and the large broad leaves and high water content become energetically too costly, if structurally not impossible, to maintain during the freezing months ahead. The conifers, of course, have chosen a different strategy. Their small and slender photosynthetic organs, or leaflets, require a minimum of maintenance during the winter.

This is the time of year when the beech trees, oaks, and hickories of the eastern deciduous forest biome are producing considerable quantities of fruit and nuts. Gray squirrels are actively foraging and caching stores to assist them in passing the winter months. At night the raccoons and opossums are busily foraging to lay on fat which will permit them to pass the worst months while eating very little. And as I enter the Zoo and cast my eye over the bears, I notice their morning activity. If they were in their natural habitat, they too would be attempting to forage, as efficiently and rapidly as possible, to lay on that last bit of fat before entering torpor and the long winter ahead.

I began work at the National Zoo some 14 years ago, and I well remember the staff meetings and the engineer's weekly report each autumn of the ground water temperature. When it reached a certain level, we always began to prepare to fire up the boilers and lay in enough coal to provide heat to the animal houses for the next four to five months. When exhibiting exotic vertebrates in a region far north of their natural origin, the problem of providing supplementary heat during the temperate zone winters is an urgent one. Now, it is true that you can have a zoo without providing supplementary heat and without building massive life-support systems in the form of "houses," but that limits a zoo to exhibiting only the fauna—whether local or exotic—adapted to the climate in which the zoo finds itself. Obviously, tropical specimens demand some form of housing during the winter.

But this very fact in part prevented the formation of large groups for exhibition. For example, if one wished to have an extensive collection of nonhuman primates from the tropics, there was some virtue in attempting to show a variety of specimens. Thus, the cages within the Monkey House would be allocated to different species. Without a conscious decision to limit the number of species exhibited, the Zoo found that space limita-

A rear view of a Milwaukee zoo exhibit shows "invisible" moats that separate animals.

tions prevented the exhibition of many troops of the same species. Since exhibiting the diversity of "God's nature" was part and parcel of the raison d'être for zoological parks, it is no wonder that large breeding groups were not maintained. It has only been in recent years that zoos have moved away from a tendency to exhibit the diversity of form and concentrated instead on showing fewer species in more natural social groupings, often with several breeding units of one species dominating the collection.

It is not only temperature which sets limits on the quantity and kinds of species that may be exhibited, but also factors of humidity and the terrain of the zoological park. For example, many species of antelope adapted to semi-arid steppe conditions do not flourish when exhibited in areas that experience a seasonally high humidity, coupled with high temperatures. Saiga antelope which roam the Russian steppes in the tens of thousands have been introduced in various zoos of the Northeast, but with little success. On the other hand, they may be exhibited to great advantage in Oklahoma and Texas. North American pronghorn antelope, while able to withstand intense winter cold, experience great difficulty in the Northeast, but thrive in Oklahoma, Texas, and New Mexico zoos.

Northern mammals may experience discomfort when exhibited in zoological parks subjected to high summer temperatures. In part, this can be controlled by providing air-conditioned quarters or by changing the diet to reduce the amount of fat laid on by the specimen during the summer months. In this way polar bears can be exhibited successfully in zoos where summer temperatures soar. Some species, such as the giant pandas at the National Zoo, cannot tolerate high temperatures and are shown in air-conditioned quarters during the summer months; indeed, a special thermometer display explains to the public whether the animals can be seen inside or outside on a given day.

Zoos in subtropical areas experience problems of a different nature, only in part related to climate. With no severe temperatures to kill the eggs and adults of certain parasites, ecto- and endo-parasite problems can become critical. In these locales, rotating animals on pasture or changing the soil in the paddocks becomes a much more rigorous routine if parasite loads are to be kept at a minimum. Biting insects in subtropical areas can also be a terrible nuisance with hoofed stock, a problem that is only temporary in the zoos of the temperate zone.

Yet no zoological garden, wherever it is located, can provide a total life-support system with a controlled environment for the exhibition of large, natural groupings of vertebrates. Therefore, a compromise is usually reached where attempts are made to show vertebrates that can stand the climate year round in large outdoor enclosures, and those that require a more exacting environment in smaller groups where they may be housed indoors during periods of inclement weather.

The subtle and not so subtle influences of climate have profoundly affected both how zoos exhibit and the size of the breeding stocks they can maintain in their collections. What follows is an excursion to several notable American zoos to see how their locale has shaped their individual characters.

THE NORTHWEST

Located on Puget Sound, between the Cascade Mountains to the east and the Olympic Mountains to the west, Seattle enjoys a rather benign climate in spite of its northern location. While many days are characterized as overcast, only 34 inches of rainfall occurs during an average year and it tends to be evenly spread. Winters are not severe, thanks to the Japan Current offshore in the Pacific. Seattle and its sister city to the south, Portland, developed late in the history of the United States because of the settlement patterns that began in the Northeast. By eastern standards, the zoological parks at Seattle and at Portland are young. The construction of moated enclosures, in fact, proceeded in advance of similar structural improvements at many of the older eastern zoos. A new noc-

161

The Minnesota zoo's Tropics exhibit, above, includes 400 plant species and 80 animal species of Southeast Asia. Center, a female white-cheeked gibbon, one of Tropics' occupants. Columns of graphics, bottom, direct visitors.

turnal house exhibits small exotic mammals by using a reversed daylight technique. Seattle has pioneered in architecture and is, in fact, the only zoo in the United States that currently has an architect as its director. Its proximity to the University of Washington has allowed cooperation to develop between the Department of Psychology and the staff. Classes in animal behavior that focus on zoo animals were developed over the last three years with considerable success. Many of these projects have assisted staff members in further research observations and improving husbandry techniques.

Portland, although the largest city in Oregon, is only about half the size of Seattle. The zoological park is correspondingly smaller but by no means inferior in ambition or quality of exhibits. Portland is known worldwide for its notable success in the captive propagation of the Asiatic elephant, a project begun some 20 years ago and whose existence has spanned the tenure of at least three zoo directors. Portland shares with Seattle a relatively mild climate for the greater portion of the year, and, situated in a lively cultural center, has received much help from the community in developing its research programs. In the mid '60s a biomedical research complex was completed to serve the interests of both the university medical community in Portland and the biomedical research community at the Oregon Regional Primate Laboratories in nearby Beaverton. The complex also initiated some early experiments and programs in the application of basic psychological techniques to the exhibition of animals. Operant conditioning techniques were employed to enhance the behavior and activities of exhibit animals. In one early project, researchers used vending machines to promote interaction between visitors and animals. Basic studies on animal behavior were initiated which continue to the present time. These programs became more valuable because of the participation of students from nearby Reed College.

THE SOUTHWEST

Southern Arizona is characterized by climatic extremes. Because annual precipitation is so low, the lowland vegetation is typified by cacti and tough, woody shrubs capable of withstanding the desiccating effects of the sun's rays. The winters turn cool indeed while the summers exhibit temperatures in excess of 105 degrees F. Yet this area is rich in native species that have developed specific adaptations for tolerating such climatic extremes. The varied rodent fauna of this lowland desert region have evolved adaptations for avoiding temperature extremes; many are nocturnal and all shelter in burrows to avoid the annual or diurnal temperature fluctuations. The mountains of southern Arizona receive more rainfall and add to the floral and faunal diversity. Representative wildlife from the Rocky Mountains include bighorn sheep, mule deer, and, in former times, even the grizzly bear.

The Arizona-Sonora Desert Museum was designed to exhibit local wildlife and plants. It differs from most zoological parks in that it makes no attempt to show a specimen from outside of the biotic province in which it is located. Yet, what with so many species of vertebrates that have become nocturnal or require burrows to avoid high temperatures, to exhibit them is a challenge. To this end, the lighting cycle has been reversed, and the visitor walks past the glass front of exhibits which are illuminated with red light. In addition to reversed lighting cycles, simulated burrows have been constructed with viewing windows in the nest chamber. In some cases the entire tunnel system has been constructed against glass, providing the visitor with an intimate glimpse into the lives of small vertebrates which would be denied the casual observer hiking through the desert. Kangaroo rats and pocket mice may be closely observed as they gather seeds or construct a nest. The ring-tailed cat is also on exhibit, affording many Tucson residents their first glimpse of this shy relative of the raccoon.

Those exhibits not enclosed in special houses or underground viewing chambers have been designed to blend in with the natural vegetation and landscape of the area, tastefully conveying to the visitor the diversity of local wildlife. The concept of introducing the local fauna of an interesting region to an urban population through imaginative exhibits stands as a model for other regions in the United States. It further points out that the exhibition of exotic specimens for their educational value should not be the sole goal of every zoological park. Rather, a glimpse into the lives of small vertebrates in any geographical region offers challenges and great educational value for the public.

Situated in large centers of urban population, Los Angeles and San Diego have been able to draw upon their community resources and become zoos of international stature. They share the mild Southern California climate, which means that most exhibits can be developed as expansive outdoor display areas and that heated quarters need be provided only during part of the year. The long periods

A beluga in Minnesota zoo's Sealife approaches window in 500,000-gallon exhibit.

163

of aridity during the annual cycle in Southern California, however, can cause range land and pastures to rapidly lose vegetation, making artificial watering and close attention to pasture rotation mandatory when keeping hoofed stock in such areas. In spite of the problems associated with the Mediterranean type of climate in general, the overhead necessary to create a life-support system for animals during the winter is minimal. The problems of constructing huge enclosed houses for exhibition so characteristic of the Northeast and Midwest are almost completely nonexistent in Southern California.

San Diego has taken tremendous strides in breeding rare and endangered species of mammals, especially hoofed stock. San Pasqual facility, outside of the metropolitan area of San Diego, has permitted large-scale husbandry of endangered ungulates. The largest herd of white rhinoceroses outside of South Africa inhabits this park. So successful are the captive propagation efforts that San Diego now is faced with the problem of dispensing with excess stock, a monumental task that may eventually involve a headlong confrontation with the practice of euthanasia.

The exhibit zoo itself, in downtown San Diego, gives the visitor a feeling of openness. The massive houses necessary in the North are absent. Moated enclosures, spacious outdoor cages, and aviaries dominate the scene. San Diego has had a long-term commitment to research with the emphasis strongly developed toward the biomedical community. This zoological park maintains the largest staff of veterinarians of any zoo in the United States, and their recently constructed veterinary hospital offers the best in treatment and diagnosis. The zoo has also had a staff pathologist in its employ for over two decades.

San Diego pioneered in barless enclosures (grottoes with moats), and has continued to be innovative in exhibition techniques. The new gorilla enclosure at San Pasqual has departed from the usual concrete grotto type and offers a splendid outdoor exhibition of gorillas on grassy turf. A strikingly designed pyramid of logs serves as an exercise area and as a resting place for younger gorillas.

Los Angeles has specialized in the captive propagation of rare and endangered species of marmosets. Most notably, the zoo has established a colony of the endangered cotton-top marmoset, *Saguinus oedipus oedipus.* The marmoset breeding facilities at Los Angeles are entirely off exhibit and represent

a unique attempt on the part of its director, Warren Thomas, to put the expertise of the zoo at the disposal of a species whose continued survival in its native Colombia is dubious indeed.

Warren Thomas had a great deal to do with the design and construction of the relatively new Gladys Porter Zoo at Brownsville, Texas where he was director before moving to Los Angeles. Enjoying the benefits of the splendid climate on the Gulf of Mexico, Brownsville is able to exhibit exotic specimens in an almost entirely outdoor setting. Heated quarters are provided, but the general effect is an outdoor zoo. Animals are confined by moats with extremely low walls and by judicious use of "hot wires" placed along the tops of retaining walls. The rather wet climate of Brownsville allows luxuriant growth of plant life in the paddocks, which are also protected by hot wires and thus remain free from depredations by the inhabitants. In terms of what a small zoo can look like in an urban area, given the appropriate climate, the Gladys Porter Zoo makes a terrific visual impact. It represents a way in which advantage can be taken of local climatic conditions to produce tasteful exhibits of exotic specimens.

THE GREAT LAKES

Quite the reverse sort of problem was faced by the developers of the new state zoo in Minnesota. With its rather severe winters and deep snows, Minnesota needed to provide the public a means of observing specimens in buildings and to move people from building to building without the inconvenience of inclement weather. In other words, the public had to be protected as well as the animals. A similar situation has been successfully handled in Münster, West Germany, which is subject to heavy rainfalls as well as high winds that blow off the North Sea. Münster, too, paid as much attention to protecting the public from the elements as it did to protecting the animals.

In nearby Illinois, Indiana, and Ohio, urbanization and industrialization proceeded at a great pace in the 19th century. Chicago early on became a major growth center. Today, two major zoological parks flourish: Lincoln Park, located in the center of the city, and Brookfield, set in a nearby suburb. Lin-

Giraffes in San Diego Wild Animal Park roam through Southern California's arid hills. These lofty animals serve as sentinels in the wild.

The train may offer the best way to view San Diego Wild Animal Park, above, which spreads out over 1,800 acres. Below, the park's Nairobi Village houses zoo-related activities.

coln Park is characterized by careful curatorial efforts to manage intensively a diverse collection in the heart of a metropolitan area. In recent years, research on the husbandry and propagation of poorly understood groups of mammals has dominated their efforts. Their most notable successes have been in developing diets and propagation techniques for anteaters, sloths, and armadillos.

Established in the late 1920s, Brookfield is the more recent of the two zoos, and its original exhibition plan included moated enclosures modeled after the Hagenbeck model. Because the Midwest is typified by very warm summers and extremely cold winters, large houses permitting the indoor exhibition of specimens are integral to the exhibit plan. So strong are the dictates of climate that the most ambitious enterprise of the Brookfield staff in recent years has involved the construction of an immense building to house monkeys and apes in a simulated rain forest. The building will be entirely air-conditioned, and the concept of outside exhibition in this case has been completely abandoned. The public will proceed through a number of walkways to view the monkeys and orangutans at various heights in the simulated forest environment. One scarcely realizes the amount of faith that has to be mustered for a unique architectural venture such as this. The animals will be fed in non-exhibit-cage areas where it will be possible to confine them and handle them for treatment. It is one thing to show animals in an open environment, but quite another to maintain control of them, even for such elementary procedures as routine veterinary checkups. The possibility of developing multispecies exhibits is also possible at Brookfield, though in practice—as at other zoos—difficult to carry out. Under confined conditions species that coexist in nature could, in fact, become incompatible. Yet the enthusiasm of the director, George Rabb, and his curator, Benjamin Beck, knows no bounds. They may well succeed.

THE SOUTHERN PLAINS

The southern plains states of Oklahoma and Texas share similar problems in combating cold winters and hot summers. Yet in the southern extension of the plains at San Antonio, the effects of cold winters are ameliorated somewhat. Furthermore, the climate at San Antonio is similar to certain parts of North Africa, so the breeding of ungulate species such as gazelles and antelopes has enjoyed marked success. Nowhere else in the United States are exotic ungulates bred so successfully and under so intensive a management regimen.

The Oklahoma City Zoo, somewhat farther north but blessed with a rather dry climate, has also had notable success in breeding hoofed stock. But it has been more innovative in exhibiting carnivores such as the African wild dog and the North American wolf. Viewing a pack of wild dogs in a spacious grassy enclosure with shade trees and brush is remarkably different from viewing the same species in a concrete moated enclosure or behind bars. Unquestionably, the finest canine exhibits in North America are now to be found in Oklahoma.

NEW YORK CITY

Located in one of the largest metropolitan areas in the United States, the Bronx zoo, managed and supported by the New York Zoological Society, has earned itself a reputation for leadership in both zoo architecture and research. Its outdoor African Plains exhibit, built in the early 1940s, is still famous for the innovative manner in which it showed lions and antelope in a northern cli-

mate. Recent construction has centered on improving the zoo's bird exhibitions.

In the 1960s the zoo exhibited sea birds behind glass and in a simulated marine environment. Auks, guillemots, puffins, and cormorants must have almost felt at home. Yet the aesthetic force of the display was nothing compared with the vast filtration system necessary to maintain purity of the water that flows through it. Particular care is taken to filter certain agents deleterious to the natural waterproofing of the sea birds. The exhibit proved a tremendous success and led to the construction and opening of the World of Birds exhibit in the 1970s, a stunning high point in the construction of artificial environments for the exhibition of exotic vertebrates. The exhibit areas are divided into different habitat types: arid, deciduous forest, tropical forests, and so on; mixed species of reasonably compatible birds live within. A walk through the World of Birds is a truly educational experience, partly because of the beautiful architecture, partly because of the brilliance with which habitats are simulated, and even partly because of the graphics, which convey the salient facts of avian biology in an imaginative, nondidactic manner.

The World of Darkness, opened in 1969, portrays mammals in semi-natural habitats with a reversed lighting system. It is one of the first exhibits anywhere successfully illustrating diverse feeding mechanisms. The intriguing exhibition of bats was in no small measure influenced by the presence of one of

The San Diego Zoological Society maintains an extensive botanical collection to complement naturalistic animal exhibits.

Revamping a federal building complex on the outskirts of Tucson, the Pima County Park opened the Arizona-Sonora Desert Museum in 1952. A desert bighorn sheep, opposite, from Sonora, Mexico, lives in a realistically landscaped craggy enclosure at the museum.

the nation's leading bat experts, Donald Griffin, who was associated with the zoo's research center during the late 1960s.

The Bronx zoo has always been a pioneer in promoting field research. This is no less true than in the days when world-famous biologist William Beebe wandered the tropics under the sponsorship of the New York Zoological Society. The laboratory building that once served as the focal point for his efforts to promote research in tropical biology now houses the field biology offices. Four staff scientists are supported by this office in their research efforts, which take place all over the globe. Although seldom in residence, the scientists have a home base here out of which to operate when they return from the field to engage in the lengthy process of grant applications and write-ups. The New York Zoological Society, through this office at the Bronx zoo, has been able to train graduate students in field biology and has actively pursued a program of training zoologists for curatorial roles in zoos. This has been done not only through on-the-job training but by funding research projects which may even take the neophyte curator

back into the field and away from the park itself. Such flexibility and imagination have always characterized the activities of the New York Zoological Society.

After this brief review of sister institutions —and with all due respect for their various economic and environmental problems and their diverse solutions—I remain encouraged over the role of zoos in the conservation movement. It is clear that all zoological parks worthy of the name must recognize the continuum from field to intensive management. Wildlife preserves such as national parks are at one end of this continuum while zoological parks with their elaborate life-support systems are at the other. Yet both have much to offer. Our own unit at Front Royal may be considered as a halfway house in the grand scheme of wildlife conservation. Those of us charged with the responsibility for intensively managed collections have an obligation to share our insights, mistakes, and successes. As for myself, I am grateful that the National Zoo as a bureau of the Smithsonian Institution has the freedom to approximate those scientific and educational ideas entrusted to us.   □

ANIMALS ALIVE

Humans since the beginning of time have sought to represent animals, to make them come alive—for our own purposes. When poorly done, this anthropomorphic cartooning reduces animals to travesties of creation: ducks in pants, bears in hats. When sublimely done, we see mastodons materializing on the firelit walls of Cro-Magnon caves, or read Rudyard Kipling's "Just So" stories. Though masterpieces, these too turn the animals into human creations.

Photography has allowed a variety of enthusiasts in modern times to enter the animal world, but with greater objectivity. Like a caveman's flint piercing the bear's heart, the successful photograph hits the target of the animal's spirit.

In that success, oddly, the photographer's art becomes one with the zoologist's science. They both dare to penetrate the animal's mystery, to probe the reality there, not through men's eyes but as it is. Ultimately they both dare speak for the animal with graphic or scientific truth.

"Two of the scariest animals in the Zoo," says General Curator Jaren Horsley of the polar and Kodiak bears under his charge. Neither of the species responds well to the kind of behavior training that elephants receive. There remains the constant possibility,

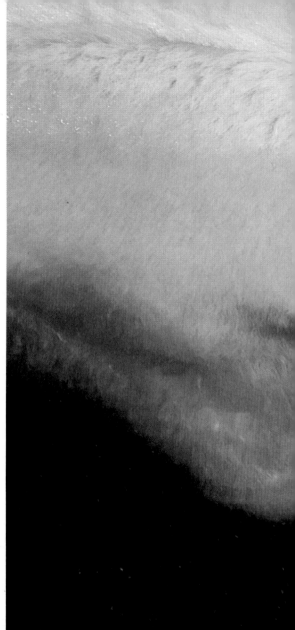

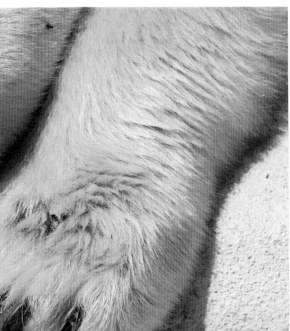

Polar bear paws work as either sun shades while snoozing, left, or paddles when swimming, above. Biggest of all bears, the massive polar bears (which may stretch out to 10 feet) have near-rivals in the Kodiaks, opposite, largest of the world's brown bears. For the first several months, infants of both species require heat and solitude.

particularly with the polar bears, that one of those massive paws might sweep a keeper off his feet, at least. Horsley perceives this unpredictability as a part of the body of scientific fact, knows that the paws grew snowshoe-broad because of the bears' need to cross pack ice for food. He worries also that the Kodiaks, members of the wide-ranging American brown bear family, are mighty vulnerable, even with their size, to the teasings and tidbits that harass all zoo animals.

The Zoo's big cats, while also unpredictable, behave a bit more docilely and on cue, assuming that they have been hand reared. Evolution has urged them to save their strength, enjoy the sun and life's other benefits between feedings. Perhaps that's why life at the Zoo lengthens the earth times of some species. Look at the beautiful, beloved white tiger, Mohini, of whom Director Ted Reed commented, "She would have been a movie star if she'd been human." She lived to be 20, possibly five years longer than an expectable life in the wild, because of National Zoo-style tender, loving care.

For what purpose? First for delighting and educating people about the wonder of these beasts. Then for understanding them better,

Mohini, bottom opposite, late matron of the Zoo's white tigers, has been followed by others of the white strain. Male and female lions, paired and pawing, share turf at the William M. Mann Lion-Tiger Exhibit, below. Jaguars, left, must stay in cages because they could leap free.

answering such questions as how they behave biologically.

Another reason for conserving animals their whole life long—a reason even beyond viewers' interest and curators' scrutiny—is the very fact of survival. White-cheeked gibbons, nearly extinct in their native, war-torn lands of Southeast Asia, thrive in Zoo conditions. Beyond their beguiling characteristic of singing morning and afternoon duets for the amazement of zoo-goers, these just-saved-from-extinction primates are monogamous. To humans, who tend to regard the trait of monogamy with special affection, gibbons therefore seem worthy of devoted research.

Regarded as most beautiful monkeys for ogling, the Roloway guenons from Africa's tropical forests also have the bizarre habit of grimacing back at folks who make faces at them. Yet, because of their good looks, they're all called "Diana," whether in honor of the classical goddess or in memory of a forgotten keeper's friend.

In the near future, the Zoo will open up a new Monkey Island exhibit in which the behavior of primates can be monitored by anyone with eyes or camera plus patience. Located there will be the Barbary apes, handsome if sorrowful-looking animals found naturally only in North Africa. Worth noting, as they break their large troops down into smaller social organizations, is how they re-

Primates flunk the colorful test, being generally black and white—like the African guenon, above, and Indochinese gibbon, right. Yet the Barbary ape, opposite top, manages a rich brown, and the golden marmoset deserves its name.

174

main tolerant of each other despite restrictions and competitive possibilities.

Less easy to observe are such rare lower primates as the slow lorises. Prosimians from Southeast Asia, they challenge Zoo display artists by their nocturnal habits and frustrate viewers by their lethargic behavior. Curators give higher priority to animals that both exhibit well and are of research value, and thus regard the eye-catching and fascinating Matschie's tree kangaroo as a preferred species. An unusual creature, seldom seen even in zoos outside its native New Guinea, it lives at the National Zoo in two places: at Rock Creek Park, where one may watch it hopping through trees in its display area, and at Front Royal's Conservation and Research Center, where scientists study its breeding and husbandry.

Birds are of another stripe. That is, Zoo keepers approach them rather differently than other animals, in part because of their relatively short life-spans. "A while back we used to regard birds as expendable," admits Assistant Director John Eisenberg. "Now we take a longer view, and treat them as important species, many of which are endangered —particularly the cranes."

How can small mammals from warm climes—the fennec, above, slow loris, right, bush baby, above right, and Matschie's tree kangaroo, opposite— wear such heavy fur coats? The fur is insulation against extremes of heat and cold.

The famous Rothschild's mynahs, examples of rare birds at the Zoo, dazzle viewers with their ballet-dress white bodies and their blue masks. In the wilds of their native Bali perhaps only 500 survive. Although the Zoo has enjoyed success in breeding them, Front Royal's Curator of Birds Guy Greenwell is concerned about the limited nature of the gene pool he's dealing with—inbreeding being no more desirable among Rothschilds than among any of us.

In the lore of the Smithsonian is the fact that barn owls once lived in the turrets of the red Castle on the Mall. Recently two Zoo-reared owls were put up there in an effort to establish them once again . . . given a correlation between the owls' wisdom and the Smithsonian's intellectual leadership. Having successfully nested, the barn owls flew away to other less tumultuous campuses.

Yet, before drawing any conclusion from this, it would be well to hear Curator Charles Pickett's generalized comments on birds: "They don't have 'personalities'; but birds do have individual characteristics that make it possible to tell one from another."

Snakes seem to exist beyond the ken of most mortals. But for an astonishing number of both amateurs and professionals, these are

Specialization in birds takes many forms, and the whys of a huge horny crest or a particular color are matters of speculation. In the barn owl, opposite left, the entire head reflects the importance of the eyes. Less easy the reasons for colors and crest of the cassowary, opposite right; the mask of the Bali mynahs, shown in combat, top; or the tuft of the crowned crane, above. The secretary bird, left, has long legs and strong wings which help it capture and subdue snake prey. Yet its name refers to the feathers at the back of the head, which recall the pencils and quills behind the ears of secretaries in days gone by.

the most interesting animals alive. They are
neat, colorful, and companionable (in the
sense that they will fit in well with apart-
ment-dwelling households, requiring only a
bathtub or some other form of moisture con-
tainer, varied types of food, and moderate
temperature). Nonetheless, snake students, at
the advice of Dr. Eisenberg, "had better com-
bine with their tender loving affection an en-
cyclopedic knowledge."

For mysteries abound among snakes. The
two very different-looking species on these
pages, by illustration, are both arboreal and
fill nearly identical niches in their separate
tropical worlds. Indeed, the emerald tree boa
(opposite) and the green tree python (this
page) both have offspring that eventually
turn green—though the boa bears live young
and the python produces eggs from which
yellow or orange young emerge. But, by a
process no one understands, a varied version
may one day come forth, such as the blue
python which is pictured below in the throes
of incubating its eggs.

How nature manages this bizarre trans-
mutation—perhaps it's a kind of reptilian
albinism—demands further study from
zoologists. Meanwhile, the photographers
simply rejoice.   □

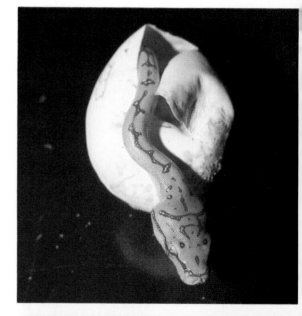

Rather than winding around a branch, emerald
tree boas are apt to hang saddled over it, right,
their large teeth ready. The newly emerged green
python, top, which will soon turn its proper color,
immediately sets about its sinuous destiny, above.

WHO'S WHO OF ZOOS

By no means a definitive list of zoos in America, as space permits no such attempt, we have also had to exclude here aquariums and private or commercial zoos. In describing major exhibits and further illustrating recent trends in zoo exhibits, we hope to inspire you to visit a zoo soon. Remember, "It's all happening at the zoo."

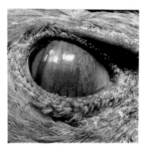

Crane hawk

Arizona-Sonora Desert Museum   Route 9, Box 900, Tucson, Arizona 85704   A living museum that displays the flora, fauna, and geology of the Sonoran Desert region only, the Arizona-Sonora Desert Museum features exhibits of bats and rattlesnakes, natural habitat grottoes for four species of desert cats, and new enclosures for beavers and otters, which once lived along the Santa Cruz River outside Tucson. A new walk-through aviary includes four separate habitats of desert birds, many of which come from Mexico. The Stephen H. Congdon Earth Sciences Center is the newest and most popular section of the museum.

Audubon Park & Zoological Garden   6500 Magazine Street, New Orleans, Louisiana 70118   The Audubon zoo offers one of the country's most exciting examples of a modernized zoological park. Warned to improve its facilities by federal authorities and humane societies in the early '70s, local organizations, corporations, and citizens displayed strong interest and a vote of confidence in their zoo by providing much-needed funds. City appropriations and federal funds also helped, and the zoo adopted and began to carry out a master plan for an expanded and imaginative zoo. Phase I, including a renovated bird house, all new landscaping, and a new entrance, has been completed, as has part of Phase II, which encompasses the major exhibit areas.

Chapultepec Zoo   Bosque de Chapultepec, Mexico City, Mexico   Located on the same site in mile-high Mexico City as Montezuma's original game reserve and thus perhaps the oldest zoo in the Americas, the Chapultepec zoo is a pleasant Victorian-style zoo with wide sidewalks and some moated exhibits. One of its most recent additions is a pair of giant pandas from the People's Republic of China. The pandas live both in air-conditioned indoor quarters and in spacious outdoor yards. Along with its strong hoofed stock and hippopotamus collections, the zoo offers elephant shows, pony cart rides, and handsome stonework on many of its exhibits. Under the same administration as the Chapultepec zoo is the new zoo in San Juan de Aragon, a suburb of Mexico City. This modern zoo features predominantly tropical and African species in large moated enclosures. In addition to these zoos, neighborhood parks throughout the city feature small, interesting animal exhibits.

Cheyenne Mountain Zoological Park   P.O. Box 158, Colorado Springs, Colorado 80901   The Cheyenne Mountain zoo, offering a panoramic view of the Rocky Mountains and the Great Plains from its 6,800-foot elevation, features a strong collection of cats and one of the

White-cheeked turaco

finest and oldest breeding herds of giraffes in the United States. The zoo has recently completed Primate World, which houses six gorillas and 13 orangutans, and exhibits birds of prey, flamingos, and wading birds. Nocturnal and pheasantry exhibits are planned.

Chicago Zoological Park (Brookfield zoo)   Golf Road, Brookfield, Illinois 60513   The Brookfield zoo features a new Predator Ecology exhibit in which animals are displayed in surroundings resembling their natural habitat. Fishing cats, for example, live beside simulated Malaysian streams, margays in a tropical forest environment, and Pallas cats inhabit a Himalayan-like terrain. Grouping its animals chiefly by species, the zoo's Seven Seas Panorama is the first exhibit of porpoises and dolphins built away from the sea coasts.

Cincinnati Zoo   3400 Vine Street, Cincinnati, Ohio 45220
The lowland gorillas at the Cincinnati Zoo, sometimes called the "gorilla capital of the world," have produced 10 babies, a world's record for live gorilla births in captivity. They are housed in a new outdoor display complex, complete with grass and waterfalls. The zoo also recently opened its Insect World, focusing on the diversity among insects and displaying many species never before kept in captivity. The zoo's Big Cat Canyon includes white Bengal tigers.

Cleveland Metroparks Zoological Park   Brookside Park, Cleveland, Ohio 44109   Cleveland's Metroparks zoo, the fifth oldest zoo in the United States, boasts a new primate and cat building featuring glass-fronted exhibits with overhead skylights that provide natural daylight for the animals. In several primate habitats, animals themselves operate push-button freshwater taps, providing them needed activity and lessening demands on keepers. A Creatures of the Night rotunda displays nocturnal animals.

Dallas Zoo   621 East Clarendon Drive, Dallas, Texas 75203   The Dallas Zoo offers a fine reptile collection, including 50 rattlesnake species, the largest number ever assembled in a zoological collection. A new desert ecology exhibit features native cacti and other succulents, as well as two dozen lizard species. The outdoor display enables the visitor to observe courtship, territorial rites, and other behaviors rarely seen by visitors. The zoo also has the largest flock of flamingos in any American zoo today, and an extensive antelope exhibit that includes miniature antelope.

Denver Zoological Gardens   City Park, Denver, Colorado 80205
The Denver zoo, which displays its animals predominantly by species, boasts two new rockwork habitats for its herds of Dall and bighorn sheep. Future plans include a new exhibition building for reptiles and small mammals, and a major aquarium with outdoor marine mammal exhibits. Bird World is one of the zoo's current attractions, with cages for different types of birds (penguins, native birds, etc.), as well as a walk-through tropical rain forest, hummingbird jungle, and aquatic bird habitats.

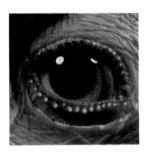

Ariel toucan

Gladys Porter Zoo   500 Ringgold Street, Brownsville, Texas 75820
Gladys Porter Zoo, which opened to the public in 1971, is laid out in five major areas, four of which are zoogeographic: Tropical America, Indo-Australia, Asia, and Africa. The fifth and only nongeographic area, the Herpetarium, houses one of the world's finest collections of

Gray hornbill

reptiles and amphibians. Landscaped as a 31-acre botanical garden, the zoo features modern naturalistic habitats on islands or in open expanses.

Henry Doorly Zoo   10th and Deer Park Boulevard, Omaha, Nebraska 68107   Overlooking the Missouri river, the Henry Doorly Zoo, which opened in 1978, is the product of a regrouped Omaha Zoological Society's efforts. The zoo's cat complex, the world's largest, emphasizes off-display isolation and management, so that more animals are actually off exhibit than on at any one time. Because of its space and management area, the zoo received a white tiger on breeding loan from the National Zoo in 1978 in a cooperative effort to produce offspring. The zoo has also placed emphasis on rare hoofed stock: its herds of gaur and Nile lechwe, an aquatic antelope, are the largest in the country; and it was the first zoo to breed bontebok. As part of its long-term breeding program the zoo maintains accurate gene pool records and careful herd family groupings.

Lincoln Park Zoological Gardens   2200 North Cannon Drive, Chicago, Illinois 60614.   The Lincoln Park zoo, perhaps America's most visited zoo, is well known for its collection of great apes, which live in family units in the Great Ape House. Erected in 1976, the building has a rain-forest environment with an outdoor warm-weather habitat complete with a waterfall. A major construction program has begun which will completely modernize the zoo by the late 1980s. New additions to the zoo will be the large mammal and hoofed stock areas, and the Penguin-Sea Bird House.

Los Angeles Zoo   5333 Zoo Drive, Los Angeles, California 90027   The Los Angeles Zoo, a completely outdoor zoo, exhibits most of its animals in five continental zoogeographical areas. Other features include an aquatics section, an Alpine animal hillside, reptile house, aviary, and large walk-through flight cage. The zoo exhibits exclusively in the United States several animal species, including the California condor, emperor tamarin, and mountain tapir. Two orangutan exhibits opened recently, as did two new gorilla habitat displays. The Los Angeles Zoo is building a fine collection of rare animals, such as its herd of Arabian oryxes. Now being constructed are a woolly monkey island, California condor flight cage, and wolf woods.

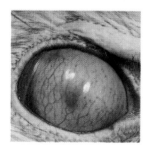

Bald eagle

Metro Toronto Zoo   Meadowvale Road, Scarborough, Canada   The new Metro Toronto Zoo, one of the world's four largest public zoos, spreads over 710 acres of forest, river valley, and landscaped open spaces in a nearby suburb of the city. Glass-roofed pavilions with naturalistic exhibits display plants and animals from six zoogeographic regions: Australia, North America, South America, Eurasia, Africa, and Indo-Malaya. Also, in the warm months the Lion Trail features African plains animals roaming freely in spacious outdoor paddocks, and the Tiger Trail offers a simulated Australian outback with Eurasian animals as well. An electric train provides sweeping views of large Canadian animals in the Canadian Animal Domain exhibit, including breeding herds of white-tailed deer and the now-protected wood bison, native to Northern Alberta and Southern Yukon. The zoo will soon offer a World of the Ocean exhibit.

Milwaukee County Zoological Park   10001 West Bluemound Road, Milwaukee, Wisconsin 53226   The Milwaukee County zoo was relocated in the late 1950s, and thus, as is the case with many renovated zoos today, exhibits animals in modern continental groupings with barless enclosures and life-like physical surroundings. Dry moats between species, such as those between the lions and the zebras, antelope and ostriches, allow predators and their prey to be exhibited seemingly together. Steller's sea lions in the North American group perform regularly, and visitors may buy fish to feed them. Along with the striking continental exhibits, the zoo offers a lush aviary with more than 800 birds, a monkey island, and primate house.

Minnesota Zoological Garden   12101 Johnny Cake Ridge Road, Apple Valley, Minnesota 55124   The Minnesota Zoological Garden has been open to the public only since May 1978. Featuring northern hemisphere species, it groups its animals zoogeographically in nature-imitating habitats. Some of the zoo's indoor highlights include Minnesota Wildlife (indoor and outdoor); the Japanese snow monkey exhibit; and the Whales/Sea Life exhibit, featuring belugas from Hudson Bay. Outdoors along the Northern Trek, such large mammals as Siberian tigers, musk oxen, and moose are featured.

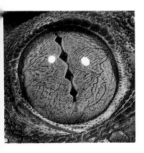

Giant day gecko

New York Zoological Park (Bronx zoo)   Bronx, New York 10406   The biggest urban zoo in America, the Bronx zoo's most recent exhibit is Wild Asia, the outdoor stage of the zoo's Asian area and part of its program to group its animals zoogeographically. Viewed from a specially designed one-sided monorail, the exhibit displays numerous species of hoofed stock, as well as Indian rhinos, Asiatic elephants, sarus cranes, and tigers. Indoor highlights include a new World of Birds, perhaps the best bird house in a northern climate; the World of Darkness; and an aquatic birds exhibit, with the only zoo breeding colony of puffins. The Rare Animals Range displays three animals now extinct in the wild: the Mongolian wild horse, the European bison, and Père David's deer.

Oklahoma City Zoo   2101 N.E. 50th, Oklahoma City, Oklahoma 73111   The Oklahoma City Zoo, currently moving toward multi-species natural habitat exhibits, is constructing a Galapagos Exhibit and planning an Amazonia Exhibit. Another future project is a 400-acre wild animal park, Africana. The zoo has the only mountain gorillas in the United States (only 12 are captive worldwide), five breeding colonies of golden lion marmosets, and the original American herd of markhor. The Oklahoma City Zoo also coordinates a national antivenin index for snakebite emergencies.

Philadelphia Zoological Garden   34th Street and Girard Avenue, Philadelphia, Pennsylvania 19104.   The Philadelphia zoo, which has been modernizing rapidly since the late '60s, opened the multi-species African Plains in 1975. It also completed outdoor enclosures for the great apes in 1977, and construction is underway for Bear Country, which, like part of African Plains, will feature underground housing or denning for the animals. The Reptile House offers an excellent collection, and the Hummingbird House was one of the first of its kind anywhere. The zoo is planning complete renovation and expansion of its Children's Zoo.

Phoenix Zoo   5810 E. Van Buren, Phoenix, Arizona 85010   The Phoenix Zoo has recently converted its exhibits from continental groupings to habitat groupings, which include forest, grasslands, and desert scrub. The new Arizona Exhibit features an open-air aviary, a museum, and indigenous Arizona animals. A young, growing zoo, the Phoenix Zoo is planning construction of elephant and cheetah exhibits. Two of its most popular current exhibits are the lowland gorillas and the Arabian oryxes, one of the world's rarest animals.

Riverbanks Zoological Park   500 Wildlife Parkway, Columbia, South Carolina 29201   Another new zoo—spring 1974 marked its opening—the Riverbanks zoo exhibits most of its animals in social units, which in turn serve the zoo's emphasis on breeding. A predominantly outdoor zoo, it houses what may be the largest breeding herd of howler monkeys in the world, a strong breeding troop of black-footed penguins, and breeding groups of saki monkeys from South America, very rare animals in captivity. A large indoor central aviary divides its species into different biotopes, such as rain forest, desert, and savanna, while hardy birds and birds of prey live outside. The zoo has bred milky eagle owls for the first time in this country.

St. Louis Zoological Park   Forest Park, St. Louis, Missouri 63110   Some of the St. Louis zoo's most impressive exhibits are the award-winning Big Cat Country; a renovated Herpetarium that organizes the reptiles and amphibians into four ecological regions and includes an indoor/outdoor wing for crocodilians and giant tortoises; and completely renovated aquatic and primate houses that feature naturalistic settings. Bird House remodeling will be completed soon. The St. Louis zoo has one of the world's largest free-flight aviaries, built by the Smithsonian for the St. Louis World's Fair in 1904. The zoo has had outstanding success with breeding black lemurs and Speke's gazelles, and features chimp, sea lion, and elephant shows.

San Antonio Zoological Gardens & Aquarium   3903 N. St. Mary's Street, San Antonio, Texas 78212   Set among natural rock cliffs and artesian springs, the San Antonio zoo is undergoing a considerable revamping, including waterfowl pools and its seal and sea lion exhibit. Meanwhile, Congo Falls provides a new home for the lowland gorillas, and the Africa Safari Walk features numerous species zoogeographically divided into various areas, such as the North African highlands, Mt. Kenya, and the African plains. The zoo also boasts an exclusive pair of breeding whooping cranes, over 30 species of rare antelope, and one of the largest bird collections in the nation, including the first flamingo colony to reproduce in a zoo.

Burrowing frog

San Diego Wild Animal Park   Route 1 San Pasqual Valley, Escondido, California 92025   Open daily in the summer from 9 a.m. to 9 p.m., this 1,800-acre wildlife sanctuary exhibits its animals in settings similar to their native habitats. A monorail, for example, offers visitors striking views of 3,000 African and Asian animals on sweeping plains and veldts. The park's crowning glory is its hoofed stock, enclosed in huge paddocks, and it has had noteworthy success as well in breeding white rhinoceroses. Hanuman langurs, Baboon Hill, and an Arabian desert biome comprise the park's most recent continental/ecological exhibits, which also include Gorilla Grotto, a tropical American rain forest, and the Native Plants Trail.

San Diego Zoological Garden   Balboa Park, San Diego, California 92112   A botanical garden of over 2,500 species of exotic plants and flowers as well as one of the largest and most diverse animal collec-

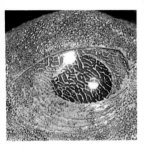

Tree frog

tions in the world, the San Diego zoo features two giant walk-through aviaries and one of the largest collections of parrots and parrot-like birds ever assembled. The zoo is the only place outside Australia to display koalas, and its zoogeographical division of animals includes new exhibits for lesser pandas and otters. Island Life displays species from Sumatra, Java, and Borneo. A Skyfari aerial tramway offers another view of this renowned open-air zoo which stretches over expansive mesas and intervening canyons.

Sedgwick County Zoo   5555 Zoo Boulevard, Wichita, Kansas 67212
The Sedgwick County Zoo opened its first exhibit as recently as 1971. Considering its population base, it spends proportionately more money on educational programs and activities than any other zoological park. This modestly sized zoo is currently divided into four major exhibit areas. The first, American and Asian children's farms, is part of an effort that will ultimately represent each continent. The African Veldt, opened in 1973, displays primarily large mammals and some primates in moated exhibits. The Herpetarium's award-winning design may have contributed to the zoo's success in breeding, for the first time in captivity, both the arrow poison frog and the green tree python. To help people overcome their fear of reptiles, this third major exhibit includes a walk-through desert biome with iguanas and other reptiles; a nocturnal gallery; and a three-level open exhibit with boas overhead in tree branches, unrestricted. The fourth exhibit, the Jungle, features a greenhouse with tropical vegetation and birds, some enclosed and moated exhibits, a vampire bat cage, and a pond with an underwater tunnel and overhead and side viewing windows.

Gray patoo

Toledo Zoological Gardens   2700 Broadway, Toledo, Ohio 43609   Founded in 1899, the Toledo zoo ranks among the nation's most complete zoos. Along with its fine collection of animals, divided predominantly by species, it offers a Museum of Health and Natural History, a greenhouse and botanical gardens, and a 5,000-seat outdoor amphitheater. The Rare Mammal Building, which houses the great apes, opened in 1978. The Toledo zoo was the first in North America to breed cheetahs in captivity and have the young raised by their mothers. It was also the first zoo in the world to artificially inseminate a chimpanzee.

Washington Park Zoo   4001 S.W. Canyon Road, Portland, Oregon 97221   The Washington Park Zoo's strongest points are its collections of chimpanzees, Humboldt penguins, and Asiatic elephants, on which the zoo is concentrating considerable educational, research, and conservation efforts. Indeed, the zoo has the only breeding herd of Asiatic elephants in the United States. It is planning to develop an elephant museum and is building a new enclosure for the elephants as well as planning one for the chimpanzees. The new penguin exhibit was recently completed.

Woodland Park Zoological Gardens   5500 Phinney Avenue North, Seattle, Washington 98103   Three major new natural habitat exhibits characterize the Woodland Park zoo. The temperate Deciduous Forest displays various birds and mammals from Western Europe and eastern North America. The Tropical Forest Island Complex features gorillas and Asian primates, and the expansive tropical grassland Africa Savanna exhibits a wide variety of African animals.

INDEX

Illustration and caption references appear in *italics*.

A

Acquisition of animals, 50-57
  costs, 52
  donations, 34, 50
  expeditions, 34, 36, 50-52, 58, *58-59*
  purchases, 50
  state gifts, 53
Allen, Jandel, *86*
American Association of Zoological Parks and Aquariums, 52
Amphibians, 54, 85
Anesthesia; *see* Immobilization
Animal behavior, 12, 57, 80, 98, 108, 110, 106-115, 116, *116*, *117*
  communication, 57, 71, 112-113, *113*, 119-120, 148, *149*
  dominance, 132, 140, 142
  followers, 107
  hiders, 107, *114*, *115*
  imprinting, 68, 144, 146
  infanticide, 122-123, *122*, 125
  marking, 142, 148, 150
  see also Maternal-infant behavior
Animal husbandry, 28, 128-151, 159
Anteaters, 93
  sculpture, *48*
Antelopes, 115, *160*, 161
  bongos, 40, 58, *58-59*, 80, 106, 107
  dik-diks, 93, 106, 107, *114*, 115
  duiker, 36
  sable, 80, *81*, 82, 106, 107
Anthony, Carter H., 34
Apes, great, 24, 64, 87, 89, 98, 166
  see also Gorillas, Monkeys, Orangutans
Arizona-Sonora Desert Museum, 163, *168*, 182

B

Baird, Spencer F., 32
Baker, Frank, 30, 34, 35
Barbary apes, 174, *175*
Bats, 167, *69*
Bears, 22, 24, 84, 160
  diet, *75*, 76
  Grizzly, 90
  Kodiak, 170, *170*, 172
  polar, 25, *35*, 42, *42*, 90, 161, 170, *170-171*, 172
  sculpture, *48*
  Smokey bear, 53
Beaver Valley, *20-21*, 70, 71, 96
Beavers, 70, 71
Beebe, William, 168
Bell, Alexander G., 34
Benson, Moses, 74
Berger, Joel, 132
Binturongs, 146, 148, *148-149*
Birds, 44, *44-45*, 77, 91, 112, *113*, 125-126, 167, 176, *178-179*
  breeding, 134-135, 144, 146, *146-147*, 178
  health care, 87, 90, 93
  keepers, 69, 135
  life-span, 54, 176
Birth control, 56, 91
Bison, *32*, 34, 156
Blackburne, William H., 30, *31*, 34, 35, 36, 84, 96
Blesboks, 93
Bluebirds, 125-126
  nesting box, 126, *127*
Boas, emerald tree, 69, 180, *181*
Bond, Melanie, 10, 11, 12, *13*, 14-15, 16, 17, 18, 64, 65
Boness, Daryl, 66, 68, 70, 96
Bongos, 58, *58-59*, 80, 106, 107
Brady, Chuck, 144
Breeding, 10-19, 28, 34, 35, 52, 68-69, 107-112, 128-137, 138-150

and animal selection, 24, 53
  birds, 127, 134-135, 145-146, 178
  eagles, 44, *45*
  exchanges and loans, 29, 38, 54-55, 140
  hoofed stock, 138-140
  inbreeding depression, 38, *53*, 55, 56, 158-159, 178
  programs, 53-57, 70, 111, 123
  see also Conservation and Research Center
Bronx zoo, 85, 156, 158, *158*, 159, 167, 168, 185
Buck, Frank, 50, 51
Buildings, 36
  Ape House, 19, 62
  Bird House, 25, 36, 45, 69, 134
  Commissary, 72, *75*, 76, *137*
  Elephant House, 36, 37, 62
  Giant Panda House, 40, *40-41*, 88
  hospital, 18, 36, 69
  Lion House, 36
  Monkey House, 26, 48, 160
  Pathology Building, 102, *102*
  quarantine building, 88-89
  Reptile House, 46, *46-47*, 64
  Small Mammal House, 10, 14, 16, 36, 64, 102
  staff, 25
  see also Enclosures, animals by species
Bush, Mitchell, *86*, 87, 88, 89, 90, 92, *92*, 93, 94, 95, *100*
  Pensi-and-Azy case, 10-19
Bush babies, *176*
Bush dogs, 70, 86, 132, 134, 142
  reproduction, 132

C

Cages
  see Enclosures
Caimans, 46
Calgary zoo, *154*
Cambre, Richard, *98-99*
Camels, Bactrian, 54, 55, 106, *109*, *129*,

130,131, 148, 150, *150-151*
Canids, 24, 85, 86, 132-133, 144, *145*
Carmichael, Leonard, 36
Cassowaries, ratite, *178*
Cheetahs, 91, *100*, 109
Chicago zoo, 156, 158
  Brookfield, 164, 166-167, 183
  Lincoln Park, 164, 166, 184
Chimpanzees, 53, 55, 64, *77*, 89
China, royal game parks, *156*
China, People's Republic of
  see Pandas
Chipmunks, Eastern, 126-127, *126*
Chrysler, Walter P., 36
Circus, 96, 157, *157*
Civets, 146, 148, *148-149*
Cleveland, Grover, 53
Climate, 35, 42, *154*, 156, 158, 160, 161, 163, 164
Cobras, king, *66*
Cody, William (Buffalo Bill), 34
Collins, Larry, 12, 132
Congress, U.S., 26, 30, 33, *33*
Conservation and Research Center, 128-137, 138-151, 158, 168, 176
  birds, 126, *127*
  enclosures, *129*, *133*, 135, *136-137*
  hoofed stock, 54, *104-105*, *129*, 138-140
  map, *130*
  staff, 25, *133*
Conservation of animals, 33, 34, 37, 52, 121, 124-125, 138-151, 157, 159, 168, 174
Conway, Kevin, 131-132
Cooper, Art, 65, 78, *78-79*, 92
Cranes, 134-135, 144
  crowned, *179*
  Florida sandhill, 128, 144, *146-147*
  Indian sarus, 144, *146*
Crocodiles, 24, 34, 46

PICTURE CREDITS

Jacket: Francie Schroeder/NZP.
Front Matter: p. 1-4 Francie Schroeder/NZP; p. 5 (top) Max Hirshfeld; p. 5 (middle) Max Hirshfeld/NZP; p. 5 (bottom) Francie Schroeder/NZP; p. 6 (top left) Pat Vosburgh; p. 6 (middle left) Susanne Page; p. 6 (bottom left) Kenneth Garrett/Woodfin Camp, Inc.; p. 6 (top right) Max Hirshfeld/NZP; p. 6 (middle right) David Kaw; p. 6 (bottom right) NZP; p. 7-8 Francie Schroeder/NZP; p. 9 Peter B. Kaplan.

Pensi and Azy: p. 10-19 artwork by Gloria Kamen.

I. Denizens:

p. 20-21 Kenneth Garrett/Woodfin Camp, Inc.; p. 22 Francie Schroeder/NZP; p. 23 (top) Max Hirshfeld; p. 23 (bottom) Francie Schroeder/NZP; p. 24 (left) NZP; p. 24 (center) NZP; p. 24 (right) Max Hirshfeld; p. 27 NZP; p. 28 Francie Schroeder/NZP; p. 28-29 (bottom) NZP; p. 29 (top) NZP; p. 29 (middle) Max Hirshfeld/NZP; p. 30-31 Library of Congress; p. 32 NZP; p. 33 SI Archives; p. 35 Library of Congress; p. 37 NZP; p. 38-39 Steve Altman; p. 38 (bottom) Steve Altman; p. 39 (top right) Max Hirshfeld/NZP; p. 39 (middle right) Francie Schroeder/NZP; p. 39 (bottom right) Pat Vosburgh; p. 39 (bottom left) Francie Schroeder/NZP; p. 40 (top) Max Hirshfeld; p. 40 (bottom left) Dane Penland/SI; p. 40-41 (bottom) Steve Altman; p. 41 (top) Francie Schroeder/NZP; p. 42-43 Steve Altman; p. 42 (bottom) NZP; p. 43 Steve Altman; p. 44 Max Hirshfeld; p. 45 (top left) Steve Altman; p. 45 (bottom left) NZP; p. 45 (top right) Max Hirshfeld; p. 45 (bottom right) Max Hirshfeld; p. 46 (bottom left) Max Hirshfeld; p. 46 (top) Steve Altman; p. 46 (middle left) Steve Altman; p. 46 (middle right) Steve Altman; p. 47 (top left) Steve Altman; p. 47 (top center) Max Hirshfeld; p. 47 (top right) Steve Altman; p. 47 (oval) Max Hirshfeld; p. 47 (middle left) Steve Altman; p. 47 (middle right) Max Hirshfeld; p. 47 (bottom left) Steve Altman; p. 47 (bottom right) Steve Altman; p. 48 (bottom left) Steve Altman; p. 48 (bottom center) Steve Altman; p. 48 (bottom right) Steve Altman; p. 48-49 NZP; p. 49 (top left) Steve Altman; p. 49 (top right) Pat Vosburgh; p. 49 (bottom left) Steve Altman; p. 49 (bottom right) Steve Altman; p. 50 Thomas J. Abercrombie ©National Geographic Society; p. 51 Theodore Reed/NZP; p. 52 Thomas J. Abercrombie ©National Geographic Society; p. 53 Donna Grosvenor; p. 54 J. Baylor Roberts ©National Geographic Society; p. 55 (top) Courtesy of The Washington Post; p. 55 (bottom) Kenneth Garrett/Woodfin Camp, Inc.; p. 56 Pat Vosburgh; p. 58 (top) Theodore Reed/NZP; p. 58 (middle) Theodore Reed/NZP; p. 58 (bottom) T. Parkinson; p. 59 (left) Theodore Reed/NZP; p. 59 (top right) Theodore Reed/NZP; p. 59 (bottom right) C. Gray.

II. Shepherds:

p. 60-62 Susanne Page; p. 63 NZP; p. 64 Susanne Page; p. 65 Francie Schroeder/NZP; p. 66-70 Susanne Page; p. 71 Francie Schroeder/NZP; p. 72 Bill Weems; p. 72-73 Bill Weems; p. 73 (bottom left) Bill Weems; p. 73 (bottom right) Max Hirshfeld; p. 74 (bottom left) Bill Weems; p. 74 (top right) Bill Weems; p. 74 (middle right) Bill Weems; p. 74 (bottom right) Susanne Page; p. 75-77 Bill Weems; p. 78-83 Susanne Page; p. 84 Kenneth Garrett/Woodfin Camp, Inc.; p. 85 NZP/Pathology; p. 86-87 Dick Swanson; p. 88 Francie Schroeder/NZP; p. 89 Mitchell Bush/NZP; p. 91 Kenneth Garrett/Woodfin Camp, Inc.; p. 92 Dick Swanson; p. 93 Kenneth Garrett/Woodfin Camp, Inc.; p. 94 (top) Dick Swanson; p. 94 (bottom) Kenneth Garrett/Woodfin Camp, Inc.; p. 95 Dick Swanson; p. 96 Susanne Page; p. 97 (top) Susanne Page; p. 97 (bottom left) Stan Barouh/NZP; p. 97 (bottom right) NZP; p. 98-99 Kenneth Garrett/Woodfin Camp, Inc.; p. 100 (top) Kenneth Garrett/Woodfin Camp, Inc.; p. 100 (details) NZP/Office of Animal Health; p. 101-103 Kenneth Garrett/Woodfin Camp, Inc.

III. Zoology:

p. 104-105 Kenneth Garrett/Woodfin Camp, Inc.; p. 106 Susanne Page; p. 107 E. Merritt; p. 108 Max Hirshfeld; p. 109 (top) NZP/CRC; p. 109 (bottom) Eugene Maliniak/NZP; p. 110 NZP/CRC; p. 111 William Albert Allard; p. 113 NZP/OZR; p. 113-114 Pat Vosburgh; p. 115-117 Peter B. Kaplan; p. 118 John Eisenberg/NZP; p. 119 Theodore Reed/NZP; p. 120 J. Elgen; p. 121 E. Hanumantha/Photo Researchers; p. 122 Rasanayagam Rudran and David Mack; p. 123 John Eisenberg/NZP; p. 124 (top) NZP; p. 124 (bottom) Mandal Ranjit/Photo Researchers; p. 125 Mandal Ranjit/Photo Researchers; p. 126 Russ Kinne/ Photo Researchers; p. 127 (top) Michael David Brown, Inc.; p. 127 (bottom) Gee Gee Snyder; p. 128 Kenneth Garrett/Woodfin Camp, Inc.; p. 129 (top) NZP/CRC; p. 129 (bottom left) William Albert Allard; p. 129 (bottom center) William Albert Allard; p. 129 (bottom right) Jan E. Skrentny; p. 130 (map) Michael David Brown, Inc.; p. 130 (top left to right) William Albert Allard, William Albert Allard, Jan E. Skrentny, Jan E. Skrentny; p. 130 (middle) William Albert Allard; p. 130 (bottom left) Jan E. Skrentny; p. 130 (bottom right) William Albert Allard; p. 133 William Albert Allard; p. 134 (top) William Albert Allard; p. 134 (bottom left) Jan E. Skrentny; p. 134 (bottom right) William Albert Allard; p. 136 William Albert Allard; p. 136-137 (top) NZP/CRC; p. 136-137 (bottom) William Albert Allard; p. 137 Jan E. Skrentny; p. 138-139 William Albert Allard; p. 140-141 William Albert Allard; p. 141 (top) William Albert Allard; p. 141 (bottom) Lucia de Leiris; p. 142-145 William Albert Allard; p. 146-147 Kenneth Garrett/Woodfin Camp, Inc.; p. 148-151 William Albert Allard.

IV. Zoo America:

p. 152-153 Kenneth Garrett/Woodfin Camp, Inc.; p. 154 (top) Lyle Rosbotham/Lensman; p. 154 (bottom) Peter Kärsten/Calgary Zoo; p. 155 Michal Heron/Woodfin Camp; p. 156 Freer Gallery of Art; p. 157 (left) Tom McHugh/Photo Researchers; p. 157 (right) Bettmann Archive; p. 158 New York Zoological Society; p. 159 (top) New York Zoological Society; p. 159 (bottom) Peter B. Kaplan/Photo Researchers; p. 160-161 Milwaukee zoo, p. 162-163 John Perrone/Minnesota Zoological Garden; p. 165 Michal Heron/Woodfin Camp; p. 166 Tom McHugh/Photo Researchers; p. 167 Michal Heron/ Woodfin Camp; p. 168 Doris Ready/Arizona-Sonora Desert Museum; p. 169 Al Morgan/Arizona-Sonora Desert Museum; p. 170 William Quinn/Lensman; p. 170-171 (top) NZP; p. 170-171 (bottom) Max Hirshfeld; p. 172 Francie Schroeder/NZP; p. 172-173 (top) NZP; p. 172-173 (bottom) Max Hirshfeld/NZP; p. 173 Francie Schroeder/NZP; p. 174 NZP; p. 174-175 Max Hirshfeld/Lensman; p. 175 (top) NZP; p. 175 (bottom right) NZP/CRC; p. 176 (left) Kenneth W. Fink/Bruce Coleman, Inc.; p. 176 (top) NZP; p. 176 (bottom right) Francie Schroeder/NZP; p. 177 D. & R. Sullivan/Bruce Coleman, Inc.; p. 178 (left) Kjell Sandved; p. 178 (right) Peter B. Kaplan; p. 179 (top) Francie Schroeder/NZP; p. 179 (bottom left) Pat Vosburgh; p. 179 (bottom right) NZP; p. 180 Trooper Walsh; p. 181 Francie Schroeder/NZP; p. 182-187 Constance Warner.